Two Hearts
in Tuva

Two Hearts
in Tuva

Wendy Taylor

MOON
BOOKS

Winchester, UK
Washington, USA

First published by Moon Books, 2012
Moon Books is an imprint of John Hunt Publishing Ltd., Laurel House, Station Approach,
Alresford, Hants, SO24 9JH, UK
office1@o-books.net
www.o-books.com

For distributor details and how to order please visit the 'Ordering' section on our website.

ISBN: 978 1 78099 341 6

A CIP catalogue record for this book is available from the British Library.

Design: Stuart Davies

Printed and bound by CPI Group (UK) Ltd, Croydon, CR0 4YY

We operate a distinctive and ethical publishing philosophy in all
areas of our business, from our global network of authors to
production and worldwide distribution.

CONTENTS

Acknowledgements

Thank you to Moon Heart – shaman extra-ordinaire. The lady continues to work her magic from another realm.

Thank you to Llyn Roberts Herrick for your valour and vision, without you there would have been no journey to Tuva.

Thank you to Mike, Gisela, Sam, Jennifer and Diane for being great companions on this memorable journey.

Thank you to my husband Barry for your unfailing love, support and encouragement in my struggle to write this book.

Thank you my reader, this book is for you with the hope that you too find the courage to follow your heart, discover the magic of the unseen shamanic world and thereby enrich your life.

Chapter 1

Well, here I was on the first leg of yet another journey into a distant land, sitting again on a jet plane on the runway of Heathrow airport, a trip that this time would be taking me all the way to Siberia.

This I knew would be a difficult and testing voyage and it was not one I was looking forward to; in fact it was with butterflies in my stomach and some trepidation, for I would not be walking a regular tourist route, but heading into the vast unpopulated areas with a small group of people I had yet to meet.

Why was I going?

Once again I had been called by the unseen spirits who frequently made demands on me... demands that in spite of my fears I seemed unable to refuse.

In my purse I had a scrap of paper on which was written an unattributed quote that I kept fingering, somehow taking comfort from it, which read, "Dreading what you're about to do is a sign that it is of great value."

Several times in the past I had set out on similar journeys beset by my fears, but I trusted in the call from my heart and unfailingly I would return from them feeling more confident and in tune with my deeper self.

Siberia! The name of this land immediately conjures up a vision of vast expanses of emptiness, a wilderness with temperatures that sink to unfathomable depths.

So many misgivings had arisen since I had committed to this trip eighteen months previously when the first mention of it had reached my ears while I was in Florida attending a workshop led by a man named John Perkins.

The workshop had been entitled *Shapeshifting* and was six days learning about shamanism. John was and still is a wonderful and generous teacher who had spent many years with shamans in the Amazon Rainforest.

The time spent with him and his assistants enforced my need to learn more from the cultures who still embraced and practiced the beliefs in this way of life, and when mention was made of this forthcoming trip I knew instantly that I must follow it up. Although I knew nothing about this country, had no known connection with it and it was an irrational thing for the middle-aged wife of a corporate businessman to do, I immediately put my name forward.

The months had swiftly passed and now as I sat on the plane at the start of this journey my mind floated back over the way my life had changed so dramatically since my first meeting with John in India, which was now over four years ago.

I pondered on the mathematically highly-impossible coincidences that had peppered my life since 1990, when for a period that lasted for six weeks I had endured a series of unsought and frightening events that pushed me into a period that is now commonly termed a 'Spiritual Emergency', a term coined by Stanislav Graf in an attempt to label mysterious, nonphysical and inexplicable events that can put the participant into deep emotional turmoil.

During this time, the experiences were beyond comprehension and defied explanation. They not only gave me the ability to be aware of dramatic events happening simultaneously in other parts of the country, but I also had foresight, the accurate knowledge of future events that would usually happen approximately twenty-four hours later.

People who I knew who were most definitely dead would appear and pass me unsought information, which would unfailingly prove to be true; several times I 'popped out of my body' and went flying across the local landscape. Even my car keys at one time literally softened and changed shape while in my hand; a few weeks later following this first incident I picked them up while in a state of anger and they twisted into a tight spiral.

It was a terrifying but also mind-blowing ability, and when after this short period of total accuracy all of this metaphysical activity ceased I was left with an overpowering need to find an explanation and a search for others who had even for a brief period also possessed this ability. My life and beliefs could never be the same again for I knew without doubt there was so much more to life than the humdrum of daily minutiae; and my visions instigated the need for an understanding and set me off on a spiritual search.

No stretch of the imagination could have envisaged what the future held for this unsuspecting housewife when the spirits came calling on that August morning in 1990. But the first stop after these bizarre experiences had taken me to the local Spiritualist Church and from those beginnings my search had spread ever outwards, and what grew into a serious quest had led me to many lands. My path had crossed with some amazing people until finally I was rewarded with meeting John in Ladakh in 1999. This man had opened my eyes to the world of animism and introduced me to shamanism.

With his guidance at his workshops in America and a couple of trips where I had joined him visiting shamans in the high mountains and also the jungles of Ecuador, I had taken a great leap forward in my spiritual education. A period that had fed my insatiable need to learn more of the mysteries of life and now for the past four years it had been focused on learning all I could of shamanism.

However, I had long ago learned to listen to my own intuitive voice, a voice that had guided me well, and although it was at one of John's workshops that I heard of this trip into Russia, he had no personal involvement in it and would not be part of the group. But it was in response to this inner voice that I had obediently put my name down as a prospective participant and before very long had paid a deposit to secure my place.

Siberia is the land where the very word shaman originated

and my interest in shamanism had been growing over the past few years, after that first meeting with John during the extraordinary shared journey in northern India.

After two subsequent trips with him to Ecuador, this interest had grown and had by now become more of a passion, one that I was constantly nurturing.

In my continuing quest for an understanding of the mysterious happenings that had begun so spontaneously and dramatically that morning over ten years ago and had continued sporadically ever since, the departure date to visit this land, where a few practicing shamans still remain, loomed ever closer.

Now as I prepared for yet another adventure I had so many fears. I had paid in full but forfeiting the money should I decide not to go was no deterrent and I would have been happy to accept this. Even at my age, I was still lacking in confidence and the concerns of making this journey were ever present.

There were so many misgivings since I had first committed myself to this trip. Why Siberia? A land that conjures up a vision of vast expanses of emptiness. I could recall flying over this area many years previously on my way back from Japan and from 30,000 feet it looked like a grey emptiness that seemed to go on forever.

To embark on such a trip was an irrational thing to do, but the deep need within me to visit this country, a place I knew nothing about and with whom I had no known connection, surpassed everything; an inner force was propelling me forward.

However, I have come to understand that as we travel through life every event or obstacle that is in our path is a means to grow towards understanding and discovering our true selves, and I knew I would forever berate myself if I had taken the easy way out, abandoned the trip and stayed at home being the conventional grandmother.

There was also an additional temptation to forfeit a sleeping bag on the cold Siberian steppes, to forgo the arduous journey through the Sayan Mountains, which had been almost overwhelming, for this same span of time clashed with one of the 'English Season' highlights, that of Royal Ascot. The indiscriminate timing meant that I would miss this premier sporting event.

For a great many years I have spent the third week of June in the Royal Enclosure at the Queen's own racecourse. Here in my finery among the silk top hats and rivers of champagne was where my family and friends expected to see me.

The aim of every horse owner, trainer or breeder of Bloodstock is to have a runner at this prestigious five-day meeting and a promising filly my husband had bred was entered in a race on the first day there. This had added further to my reluctance to leave the country and had offered a very viable excuse. But deep in my heart I knew this was a test of immense subtlety, a test from a nonhuman source. It was these unseen spirits and energies that I knew were overseeing and guiding my life and were constantly testing my commitment to this spiritual path. Now although my physical body would be absent my every thought would be with this horse as she winged her way over that hallowed turf.

In this June of 2001 my life was on the brink of yet another dramatic turn. Soon the plane had taken off and I was out over the Atlantic Ocean only hours away from America. This start to my journey was taking me in the opposite direction to my eventual destination but necessary because I still did not have a visa to enter Russia.

In New York I would meet up with Llyn Roberts who was coordinating this trip and holding this important piece of documentation. On arrival in the country I had just four hours to collect my bags, pass through immigration, to change airports and to meet up with her in order to connect with the flight that would take me all the way back over England and on to yet another continent.

In a subtle and unseen way over the past few years and in

spite of my fears, a trust that I was being guided by an unseen hand had installed itself deep within me and I was able to embark on such a journey confident that everything would unfold with perfection.

I was a seasoned traveler but concerns regarding flight delays, traffic jams between airports or even the fact that I had only once before (eighteen months previously and then only for a moment) met Llyn, and maybe would not find her in a busy airport, floated briefly into my head before being swept away and replaced by the certain knowledge that I was meant to visit Siberia at this moment in time, that it was part of my journey in this lifetime, part of my destiny and it would all work out.

The mysterious and supercharged events that continually peppered my life had, in spite of my fears, instilled such a trust that I was being guided by a unseen hand that I was left without doubt that this was where I was being called.

It was part of a relearning, a tapping into talents and abilities I felt I must have learned and held in past lives, a belief that in itself I would have instantly dismissed for the greater part of my life. But now, in spite of my strict Roman Catholic upbringing, I was able to embark on such a journey confident that everything would unfurl with perfection.

Now as I sat on the plane, and as if to reinforce my confidence, I briefly recalled just one of these incredible events.

It was during the period when what appeared to be a giant television screen would suddenly appear in the air in front of me and a scene would unfold where I would be shown events that were taking place simultaneously elsewhere in the country, and once it was the horrific murder enactment of a young woman.

Although this was inexplicable and terrifying to witness, there was an innate knowing that I had a role to play and in spite of a natural reluctance stemming from a fear of derision, I went directly to the local police station and reported all I had seen.

A few days later an incredulous police officer called to inform me that all I had told him had sadly actually taken place, even to discovering that the CD of the piece of music that I reported hearing being played (as I had watched this scenario unfold) still remained on the CD player. The description of the man I had given fitted the boyfriend who the evidence suggested was the perpetrator, a fact verified months later when a court found him guilty and he was sent to prison for many years.

So much else had happened, and slowly over the years I had discovered that I was a channel for powerful healing energies and many miraculous cures seemed to occur after I had been mysteriously guided to meet up with and connect to women who had cancer. I had not entered on this path willingly, but cautiously and reluctantly for there was no holistic background or training that directed it but so much happened that seemed to inexplicably direct me, and slowly I learned to accept this unearned talent and the fact that I was undoubtedly a channel.

Eventually the door to shamanism had been opened, which felt like a homecoming and now I was on a quest to try and understand and learn as much as I could about the people who followed this path and still practiced this ancient form of healing.

Previous to the step onto a shamanic route I had simply been following my heart in the search for an understanding of the non-ordinary events that filled my life. Events that were unsought and extremely puzzling. And it was only when my path had crossed with that of John Perkins that some sort of clarity began and slowly there came an inkling of comprehension of what was occurring.

To begin with, in the very early days I had attended Spiritualist Church meetings, joined regular meditation circles, visited psychic fairs, had tarot readings and checked out countless 'fringe' beliefs. My quest in these previous years had also taken me on travels through Egypt and India as well as into jungles and up mountains in the far reaches of our planet.

Constantly I was searching and had spent countless days exploring the ancient and prehistoric sites that pepper the English landscape, my native home.

But it was only on discovering shamanism that I felt I was finally drawing closer to an understanding of what my life was really about, why I was here and what my purpose was.

I knew the trip to Siberia that I was now setting off on would, once again, be far removed from a normal tourist excursion. There would be no meandering around familiar landmarks, no stay in comfortable hotels where showers and meals come as an inclusive part of the package.

The prime purpose of this journey was to find and hopefully witness some remaining shamans performing their healing rituals; and in several e-mails Llyn had warned our small group that we would need to travel long distances to fulfill this quest. This was a voyage to discover and hopefully share the wisdom and knowledge of the indigenous people who inhabit these lone regions.

Traditional working shamans reside these days in remote pockets of the world and are a diminishing breed, and I was clutching at any opportunity to connect with them and learn, regardless of the hardships this task continually threw at me.

There was a growing feeling that it was my duty, a role I had chosen for this lifetime, and this needed to be fulfilled. I knew with every decision the choice was still mine; no one was forcing it upon me but deep down inside me I also knew I just had to do it. There was an unspoken personal responsibility, and if I shirked this call now in my later years it would surely become a source of much regret.

So many thoughts were running around in my head as the plane carried me ever closer to the American shores. Thoughts that were laced with a sense of trepidation. The hours passed rapidly and before long we were landing at our destination. Once I had completed landing formalities at Newark, passed though immigration and picked up my bags, I made my way to JFK airport, thankfully arriving in good time. Here I relaxed slightly. I could go no further and I loitered close to the check-in desk for Moscow waiting for Llyn to turn up with the elusive visa.

I had attended workshops teaching shamanic techniques in both England and America in my desire to learn, and every time I had departed from these events with a feeling of empowerment and a joy at meeting like-minded people. Sadly none of the friends that I had met at these gatherings would be on this Siberian journey.

Llyn is a much-traveled American. She is an author and shamanic intuitive and energy healer of many years. At one point she was a psychology intern with indigenous people, going on to study Buddhism, Naturopathy and Yoga in India before becoming a practicing psychotherapist. Although she was married and at this time had two small children, she still managed to facilitate expeditions to meet both Mayan and Ecuadorian shamans and engage in shamanic intensives in the high Andes.

The only connection I had with the other six members of the team was the fact that they were either members of Dream Change Coalition, the non-profit organization founded by John, or members of Sacred Earth Network, an operation holding similar views to DCC and who were co-organizing this trip. It was with Bill Pfeiffer, the head of this trust, that Llyn had already made two recce journeys across the Russian continent and down to the Mongolian borders prior to setting up this trip for fee-paying participants.

Although I had been given the names of the other members of our small group that I was now about to meet up with, I had never met any of them and had no idea what they looked like. These people who would be my traveling companions for the next two weeks – we would be in such close proximity that I knew by the end of this time we would all know each other intimately.

In my wallet I carried a colored photo cut from a magazine article as an additional aid for identifying our leader. The picture showed just the head and shoulders of a lady with a big smile and an explosion of beautiful auburn hair. I pondered on how I would relate to her but I found the few notes of her biography on the DCC website impressive.

I checked our flight departure and saw that it appeared to be due to leave on time and found myself a seat where I could remain in view of the desk, but this was as far as I could get. The elusive Russian visa was still not in my passport and still with the courier, so for now all I could do was be patient and wait. At this point I was still longing to jump on the next plane back to England and trying hard to suppress the secret desire that she would fail to turn up.

It was an hour after the prearranged meeting time that Llyn finally and breathlessly arrived.

Profuse in her apologies for being late we joined a now short check-in queue and then she said, "Where are the others?"

I had to admit that after approaching a couple of members of the public that looked possible candidates and receiving a negative response, I had chosen to just sit and wait.

"I wonder if they have already checked in," she said. "It's possible as they already had their visas. Do you mind staying in line while I see if I can find them? I'll be back before you get to the desk."

"No problem," I said, surprised at the sense of relief I was feeling that she had arrived.

As I turned and watched her disappear into the crowd my thoughts focused on something she had been wearing. In the few moments that she had stood in front of me my eyes had been drawn to a piece of jewelry hanging around her neck. It was a simple piece of soapstone suspended on a cord, a curled cat, not a domestic one, but of the large, wild variety. Somehow I felt there was something special about it and I tried to squash a surprising rise of envy as I lusted after it. Instantly I was ashamed and embarrassed by my avaricious thoughts and banished them from the moment.

In the old movies it was de rigueur to wear a red rose as a sign of recognition. These days we just seem to say, "Meet you at the departure gate," and invariably it all works, but I must admit I had been beginning to panic. True to her word, and just as I reached the front of the line, she returned saying, "There is no sign of them. I guess they have already gone through."

She passed over my visa, we were checked in without a problem, relieved of our cases and then we quickly made our way to the departure lounge where she soon spotted two of our group.

Once she had made the introductions she said, "Bill will not be coming. With such a small group we felt it would not be necessary to have two coordinators, so he will be at home manning the telephone and be the hub should any problems arise prior to us all leaving Moscow. Already we have one hitch as Sam, one of our participants, has had her flight up to New York cancelled, so she will be coming on tomorrow and hopefully catch up with us without any further delay."

I now took stock of the two people I had just met, aware that over the next two weeks I would be sharing some intimate moments with them.

There was Mike, a man in his forties, trying to find some comfort on the small linked plastic seat, his long legs stretched out to one side. He had immediately volunteered a little of his biography and within minutes had mentioned his wife and two children who were now both away at college. His family were obviously the main raison d'être in his life and his words reflected a very masculine way of marking his territory and denoted a secure relationship in that area. I instantly felt he was a man of compassion and that his relaxed manner concealed a tower of strength. This was a good one to have on such a trip, even more so now as he would be the only male.

Seated alongside him was the third member, called Diane, a lady of middle years; she was small and stocky with thick white hair. It was extraordinary; as soon as she uttered her first few words I knew she would provide me with my 'wall'!

Generally a first meeting between strangers is a run of the mill occurrence provoking no strong emotions, but a small percentage of these first impressions will run to extremes. It couldn't have been anything she said, for the feeling was instantaneous. I hoped sincerely that I did not reveal it but there was on my part a lack of empathy, a feeling the portcullis had come down, a symbolic act of self-preservation.

There is a quote of the Dalai Lama that I try to hold close for this wise man says, "We should be most thankful for those we love least and learn to love them the most, for these are the people who give us our best lessons, for they show us where our faults are as they hold up a mirror for us."

But for now his words of wisdom were beyond my range as I tried to push a feeling of irritation to the back of my head. This instant emotional reaction to a person is one of the issues that convince me that there is so much that remains unknown.

Have we, as so many people believe, had past lives or is there instead a cellular memory? Or maybe it is held in the unseen energies that surround our body, in a field described as morphic resonance as advocated by the scientist Rupert Sheldrake.

This could explain how we all at one time or another have felt an instant empathy or adverse feeling to a person that we have never met before. How else can you explain it? Often this feeling runs deep and many times there comes this immediate deep mutual bonding and the feeling that we have known each other for eons; with it comes a complete trust in this person, a sense which over the years has never betrayed me.

Equally there are those who for no obvious reason can trigger an adverse reaction. Does this feeling result from past life memories, is this meeting an agreed set up to give the opportunity to resolve these differences and learn to love each other? So many mysteries to our lives.

All dogmas and every religion ever founded advocate the need to love our fellow man. My intention and focus in embarking on this journey to Siberia had been to learn about shamanism, but this meeting with Diane reminded me how much else I had to learn.

Embarkation began and we all found our seats, but before we left the ground there was a long delay. For security reasons a piece of baggage already loaded into the hold had to be removed as one passenger had failed to turn up.

What a nightmare for the ground baggage handlers. Imagine heaving heavy suitcases around in the middle of a New York summer, with over two hundred passengers, just searching for a specific identifying tag! Finally the captain informed us of their success, but added apologetically, "Unfortunately, there is now a long line waiting for take off and we are at the furthermost point from the runway. It will be another hour before we get airborne."

So strapped in our seats we practiced the art of waiting. Unknown to us this turned out to be a dress rehearsal and the beginning of a two-week lesson in patience, for shamans spend a great deal of time just waiting for the right moment.

At this stage I knew there was no opting out and I finally became very relaxed and began to look forward to seeing whatever lay in my path. Another adventure lay ahead and this time my search was taking me even further around the world. I knew where the plane was headed but there remained the unknown quantity as to what was in store. The search was continuing into the Russian hinterland, this unstoppable search of mine that seemed never ending and still remained unfulfilled. I slept intermittently on the long flight to Moscow, but during this time I kept getting flashes of Tibetan mandalas. It was like looking through a kaleidoscope but these patterns were forming on the ground, dirt colored, and then as I watched them they would move, change shape and then suddenly become brilliant with multi-hued color. They were incredible and amazingly beautiful and reminded me of the sand mandalas made by Buddhist monks.

Into these short naps there also came another vision which was that of a large grey wolf. In our culture the use of the word imagination covers such things, but what is imagination? For me it is a view into a different reality for I see things as clearly as if they are solid and right in front of me. This one was so real that I felt if I put out my hand I would feel the hair on his coat and the warmth of his body. Maybe I was having a glimpse of what shamans call a 'spirit guide'. I saw Llyn and myself stood a short distance apart and this wolf was moving continually in a figure of eight pattern around and between us with his head down in a purposeful walk.

A handful of times in the past few years I have had visions of this same animal, always so vivid and detailed, and if he was put in a pack I could identify him. I tried to catch his attention, to communicate with him, but he ignored me and continued to make a clockwise circle around one of us, and counterclockwise around the other linking these two circles and totally focused on what he was doing.

Finally we landed and a second lesson to test our patience came as soon as we deplaned; for there was a two-hour wait to clear Russian Immigration. In a dark, soulless building we stood en masse, slowly funneling through the one turnstile waiting for the all-important stamp to authorize our entry.

There was just one desk with one lone clerk. A hefty woman sat there devoid of expression, scrutinizing every page of every passport before stamping down her mark of approval.

Eventually we were all through, we collected our cases and

passed through into the crowded arrivals hall where we were to meet up with two other people who were part of our group; and hopefully also waiting for us would be our interpreter who would be traveling with us through out our stay.

As we walked out Mike said, "You'll spot Jennifer if she has still got the same hair style."

No sooner had he said this than out of the crowd we heard a great yell, "Miiiikkkkeeeee!" and this bundle of energy threw itself at him.

Jennifer was a girl you noticed. Even without the amazing hairstyle Jennifer would always be a girl you noticed for she contained a joy and exuberance that radiated.

We would all discover she loved people and she loved life. She was small and dark haired, in her mid-thirties and she dressed as her temperament dictated. Her hair proved the focus of attention for most of the people in that hall for it was an explosion of dreadlocks.

This style originated in the Caribbean and at the time was popular in areas of London where there is a high West Indian population, but I doubt it had ever been seen in Moscow before. Not only did she have this matted hairstyle, which today was tied up in three bunches, one above each ear and one giving her added height by sitting like a bird's nest on the top of her head. She was also tattooed!

Not for Jennifer was the discreet butterfly on the shoulder. She was a girl who threw herself wholeheartedly into every venture and the shorts she was wearing displayed a selection of the tattooist's talents.

Mike was very happy to see her; it appeared they had shared one of the intensive shamanic training sessions that Llyn facilitates in South America. These teachings had been held in Ecuador only two months ago and proved to be an empowering week for both of them.

I understood their enthusiasm and the deep respect that their visit had engendered; three years ago I also had made two visits to this same community.

On these intensives, small groups spend each day with the Tamayo family. These renowned shamans, the father Don Esteban and his two sons, Jorge and Jose, reside in Ortovalo, a beautiful place high in the Andes surrounded by three volcanic mountains. The peaks of Mojanda, Imbabura and Cotacachi dominate the landscape and are some of the sources from which these men draw the power to heal.

Their methods are dramatic and effective. A tangible energy is felt simply by watching them at work for they use the spiritual power embodied in the elements in their healing practice.

Trago the local alcoholic brew is used to cleanse the patient, but not by gently wiping the nude body standing in front of them. No. Instead they use a lighted candle and by blowing a mouthful of this liquid through the flame they engulf the patient in a fireball. They transform themselves into volcanoes, they shape shift, and in so doing the power of the flames becomes a cleansing agent.

The Tamayos also incorporate into the healing process water from the springs and use treasured sacred stones that have been passed down through the generations. Vigorous 'beatings' with stems from special plants are part of the treatment and all part of an ancient and proven ritual.

Such is their success that their reputation has spread to many parts of the world. And now, along with a patient line of men, women and children from the local area, will be those who have taken a plane journey in the search of a cure for a variety of ailments.

It was on the strength of this trip that Mike and Jennifer had both decided to pursue their studies further and on their return to the USA had immediately signed up for the excursion to Siberia.

Two other women were standing to one side also waiting for

us. One was a smiling Russian lady called Valentina who was to be our interpreter and escort while we were in Moscow.

The other member of our party stood alongside her. In appearance and demeanor she was the total opposite of Jennifer. Tall and slim, with a large amount of grey and dark streaked hair tied neatly at the nape of her neck, she had held back for a moment quietly observing. Now she stepped forward and introduced herself, "I am Gisela. Hello." Her accent was unusual and later we would learn that this lady was of German origin, but had lived in Canada for many years and was now a Canadian citizen.

Together we moved through the busy airport building and out into the sunshine. It was a beautiful day, hot and still.

The first impact the country made on me was how green it was, for this was totally unexpected. This was a tree-lined airport, where not only was the perimeter fence tree lined; there was lots of greenery nestling close to the concrete terminal buildings. With a second look I was instantly aware of the poor state of repair that everything was in. The arrivals area had large patches of missing and broken tiles on an uneven floor, and outside there were big holes in the pavements and roads; all was decrepit, grey and dirty.

The vehicle transporting us to our first overnight stay was, however, smart and comfortable but on closer inspection turned out to be German made. An hour's drive took us along a heavily congested main road; however, the road seemed to have been cut in a straight line through a forest, for on either side for most of the way stood dense, sentry-like fir trees.

Of Moscow's three airports, maybe this one stands on the perimeter of the city and we were now heading further outwards away from the metropolis.

We were all tired. For four of us there had been many hours of traveling before we had even reached New York City so there was little conversation as we covered the first few miles on

Russian soil, but Jennifer who had arrived in Moscow a couple of days earlier prattled on. We were all content to listen and I was grateful at not needing to make an effort to contribute for there was so much going on in my head as a mixture of pictures were swirling around.

The name of the first hotel we were staying in was the Golitsyn Educational Center. It was a large and grand looking building approached by a long driveway which, apart from the charmless receptionist who handed out the keys, appeared to be empty.

"Just put your bags in the room then we'll meet up downstairs," said Llyn. "I'll get us some bottled water and see if we can get something to eat."

Our group had been given four adjacent rooms; Mike was on his own and the rest of us doubled up. The rooms were at the end of a long dismally lit corridor and at the furthest point from the elevator. They were sited on the third floor which was also the top. It was a mystery as to why we had been given these rooms for the hotel appeared to be empty, but we didn't question it. We were all weary and it would only be for this first night. Although very basic they were clean, the showers worked and the water was hot, although the one towel allocated to each guest was the size of a large face cloth!

Gisela and I were sharing and I laughed when she held up this square of toweling against her six-foot frame.

With all of us feeling hungry, we soon gathered downstairs. There was no sign of either other guests or staff; the place seemed deserted. We were discussing how soon we should eat when Valentina joined us. "Ah," she said. "Dinner is from seven to eight. We will meet at seven."

This was another three hours and in the meantime there appeared to be no chance of getting either a sandwich or hot drink. Valentina disappeared again and with a lot of persuasion she found a member of the staff who reluctantly moved behind the bar and decided that it was probably possible for us to purchase either a carton of orange juice or a beer.

We survived until seven when we entered the dining room. We were, as we suspected, the only residents and a meager meal was delivered by a frozen-faced waitress; but at a few minutes to eight, as we were sitting talking, we were asked to leave.

Apparently dinner from 7 to 8 means just that, you enter the restaurant at seven and you must leave by eight! Such was our first introduction to the vagaries of hotel living in Russia in 2001.

Chapter 2

We all went early to bed and I lay down needful of a lot of sleep. But as soon as my head hit the pillow it became filled with vivid images and scenes from other trips I had made over the years. Now, strangely, in spite of the many countries I had visited, all of what I was seeing and re-experiencing, as with the glimpses of mandalas on the plane, had a strong Tibetan connection.

First I was transported back to Ladakh where I had been three years ago and I found myself once again inside the house of a Tibetan lady living there who was a well-respected shaman. This lady had been exiled from the country of her birth and was residing close to the mountains that encircled the Land of Snow; and now in the middle of the night I relived this occasion with such clarity it was as if I was actually back there. I could feel the heat of that day, hear the sounds and my nostrils filled with the smells of that moment. These sensations accompanied all of the images in front of me, full and in perfect detail.

This had been a very special day for it was the day of Wesak. A most important day for Tibetans for it is the day when the birth, death and enlightenment of Buddha are celebrated as one event. It is the most important festival in the Buddhist calendar and held on the day of the May full moon.

Prior to our visit to this lady shaman's house we had sat on the dusty ground of the local football playing area, listened to a speech by His Holiness the Dalai Lama and been beautifully entertained by the music and dancing that had followed, before walking through the dusty streets of Leh to this shaman's house. Now I relived that day when during our meeting with this shaman I unexpectedly and for the first time shifted into a strange trance. One that years later I would learn was described as a 'shape shift': a word that shamans use to describe the moments when the spirits use a living, human body as a means of channeling healing energies.

I also recalled how on that extraordinary day my eyes had physically changed color.

All of this had been tucked away in the archives of my memory. Why now, on this first night in Russia, should it have been brought so prominently to the fore?

I pulled myself back into wakefulness, I had no idea what the time was but it was still dark. I padded my way to the bathroom, but it was all very odd. I could 'feel' Tibet all around me. I kept reminding myself I was in Russia; but a powerful sense and energy of Tibet enveloped me and remained.

The logical, rational, Western trained part of me moved in rapidly. "This is nonsense. Let it go!" my brain ordered. I tried to comply and provide some equanimity by focusing on my home in England, and I pictured myself sitting on the floor playing with my grandchildren.

"Okay. You are in Moscow," I reminded myself firmly as I climbed back into bed. "Now go to sleep." But as I lay down another image instantly floated in. It was so vivid and so much more than a mere memory.

This time I was transported instantly into the Amazon Jungle, to a precise moment and it was a repeat of an experience that had occurred on my first visit there, but one that was now almost three years old.

It had been a powerful event at the time, but not one I had dwelt on, and this too had been tucked away in the recesses of my memory. My life was continually being filled with extraordinary happenings and I was constantly traveling, meeting new people and searching for an understanding of the metaphysical.

I lived very much in the present.

Without warning, a repetition of what had occurred during a short but powerful moment in the Jungle, during the brief few minutes while I was waiting for the effects of the ayahuasca I had taken to come into play. Now inexplicably there was a repeat of that experience; it had suddenly started to happen all over again.

Here in the middle of the night, as I lay in my bed on the outskirts of Moscow, I felt my body begin to swell. Then, as this tangible sense of it physically growing continued, my body filled with the powerful energy of what I recognized immediately as the Tibetan deity the Maha Kala.

There was no mistaking the presence of this force that is held in the highest regard by so many in the East. The image of this deity, one of the so-called 'wrathful gods', is frightening for he is depicted as either black or red and has huge claws extending from the fingers at the end of his four arms. Blood drips from his fanged teeth, and he has three bulbous eyes, the third being in the center of his forehead; and on his head he wears a crown of skulls.

It was all exactly the same as it had happened in the Ecuadorian rainforest, but for now it went no further and just that part of the previous experience repeated itself.

This sensation lasted for several minutes before there was a subtle shift when, like a plug is pulled, I felt a change in the balance of the energy and slowly it began to subside and withdraw. Soon it was totally gone.

I lay there for a short while totally puzzled and confused. I had no idea where it had suddenly come from or why, but there was not the slightest doubt that this deity, sometimes known as Yama, had made its presence felt.

I fell into a dreamless sleep and the next thing I knew were the first intimations of a new day, the room was growing light and morning had arrived.

I was ready for my first full day in Russia, but my thoughts were full of the Tibetan deity that had made such a forceful presence in the middle of the night, the same one that I had encountered in both Ladakh and Ecuador, but never since... He was once again making his presence felt very strongly. What could it mean?

Gisela was still asleep, so without disturbing her I quietly put on some clothes and slipped out of the door. I walked through the long, dismal and strangely quiet hotel corridors. There was neither sight nor sound of any other person and I went out into the garden without seeing a soul.

It was a warm and glorious morning, the sun had just made its presence known and the air carried the sound of birds singing to greet this new day. It took only a short walk from the building to realize that the hotel was set in what had once been stunning gardens, but now sadly were much neglected. The shrubs were untended, the lawns uncut and pathways full of weeds and holes. On one side of the building there were the remains of what had been a water garden. Its central piece had obviously been a large fountain made from intricate pieces of brightly colored glass mosaic. Now sadly large parts of it had fallen off and still lay untouched where they had fallen. A channel that must originally have had the same decorated finish, and one that would once have had a clear stream of water flowing along it, now held just dried leaves and dirty pieces of paper. This beautiful sculpture designed and built by craftsmen stood as a sad and forlorn testament to glorious days now long gone.

During this early morning stroll I tried hard to block the sensations of the night and to focus on the present, to ground myself and be aware of where I was and of all I was seeing on this first morning in Russia.

It was extremely difficult, for the pictures in my mind's eye were dominating my thoughts and all I could see were the snow-capped mountains of Tibet and images of Tibetan faces.

Try as I might I was unable to distance myself from these powerful thoughts. The energies were building and I could feel the immense power of the fearsome Tibetan deity, the Maha Kala, shadowing me. The image was both in front of and behind my eyes.

Eventually I went back inside the building and walked into

the dining room where I found the rest of the group gathered around a table; again they were the only people in the room and they were sitting in the hope of some breakfast. An absent Valentina was away in search of some staff and I sat down and joined them in casual conversation, hoping that there was nothing visible in my outer appearance, anything that would betray the disturbing state I was in; and I prayed that eating some food would ground me.

Valentina returned carrying a basket of bread rolls and the assurance that some eggs were being cooked. There was some muttering among my American companions. Coming from the Land of Plenty and not seasoned travelers they, through no fault of their own, had no comprehension or experience of food deprivation. I could see that the journey we were just setting out on was going to test all of us in so many various ways.

I picked up a roll, broke a piece off and popped it into my mouth, but I couldn't swallow it. I chewed it around. There was nothing wrong with the bread. It was my throat; there was a constriction in it and I simply could not swallow.

My whole body now was starting to tremble. These strong energies around me were continuing to build and they vibrated around and through me. It was nothing I had sought nor did I understand what was happening, but my head was filled with an image that I was unable to erase. This powerful force with a Tibetan association was something that had arrived with a total unexpectedness. It was something I had not sought, did not understand and was not welcoming.

It was confusing and frightening.

So many times over the past years I had been exposed to these strange sensations and the logical part of my brain always battles with them, constantly reminding myself that I am just an English grandmother. For there is nothing in my background or upbringing that could have set me on such a strange and mystical path.

But as always, with things that are metaphysical, by their very nature they override all logic and take precedence. I had over the past years learned it was pointless to either fight or detach myself but that I should try to become a bystander and to start by merely viewing the events that experience had told me would begin to unfold.

Llyn soon excused herself and left with our interpreter to check on our ongoing flight to Abakan; and also to seek confirmation that Sam, the last member of our group, would have arrived in Moscow and transferred to its second airport in time to connect with this. We all had our problems and our leader also had a lot of responsibilities. The rest of us remained where we were. Jennifer was in full flow and regaling us with stories from her trip to the Andes. Mike contributed a little but the other three of us remained mostly listening. I couldn't trust myself to speak for my thoughts were concentrated on containing the physical aspects of the unseen force that held me in a vice-like grip. It was like trying to hold a caged animal, and there was a fear that if I removed my focus from it something unwanted and out of control would literally escape.

Before long Llyn was back. "It all seems in order," she said. "Hopefully Sam's flight will be on time and she will make the transfer across Moscow to their other airport without a problem. The plan is to meet her there and all proceed on down to Abakan together.

Let's find somewhere nice outside where we can talk and start to bond as a group. We are going to be sharing a special time here."

Selecting a place in the shade of a tree, we formed a circle and sat down. There was still no one else around and it was wonderfully quiet; no sounds of traffic or intrusion of music and we began to believe we were the only residents of this large hotel. The staff were minimal and kept well out of the way, showing a reluctance to provide any service.

Llyn produced a ball of string and as she sat toying with it she explained what she wanted us to do.

"What we are going to do is this... Each of us in turn will share a little of our personal history, then say what has led us to this point, why we are on this particular trip and what we hope this trip will provide."

She continued, "I will start. Then keeping hold of the end of this string I will throw the ball to someone else who will contribute his or her part. They must also keep hold of the string as they throw the rest of the ball on and we'll continue like this until we have all told our story."

Llyn divulged the heartfelt desire that she had held for many years to visit Siberia. She told of how over the past couple of years synchronicities had led her to make two reconnaissance trips to this land that was calling her, of her feeling that she would be cementing her ties with this country and that part of her destiny was to work with Siberian shamans. She also shared a moment that had occurred on her last trip when she was in the village of Berdag, a small community in Tuva and close to the Mongolian border.

We sat listening in rapt attention to her words.

"As soon as I arrived there, I felt I was returning home. There was a familiarity to it and I knew where everything was and it was beyond question that I had lived there before. At one point the village shaman said she would take me to the river. But I led the way through the woods straight to the point where they had planned to take me."

Lyn then threw the ball across the circle to Mike.

He deftly caught it and held it in his hands and with his head down looking at this ball of twine he thoughtfully turned it in his hands before beginning to speak. Before he started his head came up and he slowly looked around the circle at each one of us, then he commenced. "I am an author and a psychotherapist, registered in the state of Colorado and I am also a student.

At present I am working on my Master's thesis at Regis University in Denver, which I love doing. The thesis title has to do with the recurring motifs and themes in the world's wisdom traditions. We must trust ourselves to believe that the light for which we are searching is our own light. Atman is Brahman as the Hindus say, or as the Greeks put it 'Know thyself'."

He continued, "There is nothing rational about finding myself on DCC's trips. There is only longing that seems to be met by possibilities that suddenly come into view. I first discovered the DCC website after a conference in which I was scheduled was cancelled.

I cried for joy. Really!

I never knew it would be possible for me to travel with supportive and caring people to places of which I had dreamed. Somehow, some way, we know, just know where we should be."

His eyes dropped back to his hands.

Stillness descended on the group as we absorbed the intense feeling and wisdom of this man's words.

Keeping hold of the string that connected him to Llyn, Mike looked up and with a smile sent the ball flying through the air to Jennifer.

Taking a deep breath she started and the words came pouring out of her. Her narrative was so obliquely different but no less sincere for Jennifer's aim was to heal the world.

As she sat there in the morning sunshine, it rapidly became clear that her appearance was in sharp contrast to the essence of her being. This morning she was wearing a skimpy strapless black top above thick dark blue jeans that had been cut off above the knees, leaving a ragged frayed edge. The microscopic top revealed even more tattoos. They sat on both her shoulders, and visible on her lower back in the gap between the two items of clothing were several big yellow flowers. Her feet were encased in heavy black boots laced halfway to her knees and the outrageous hairstyle topped it all.

It was extraordinary! Her outward appearance totally belied all of her spoken desires and hopes. What complex people we all are.

The words this young woman spoke were full of compassion and for sure came from the heart. They divulged a deep love for everything both animate and inanimate, and a desire to protect and nurture the earth and all that was on it. Her daily life was devoted to this end for she ran a company called Heal the Earth, and she was engaged in promoting products made totally from natural sources.

She concluded her sharing with the words, "You know, many of my tattoos are symbols that have always been used by shamans and the number 16 means peace, patience and prosperity."

The ball of string went next to Gisela and as we listened I felt that all of us were spokes of one wheel and that this voyage into Siberia was the hub that joined us all.

Her story went like this: "I was sixty-five this year. I went through World War II as a child, where I lost my father and all my uncles and grew up in a women-only world. This taught me early on that women can do everything that needs to be done and also be everything they want to be. Therefore feminists have always been an enigma to me. I haven't a clue what the hell they are talking about! I find men no better and no worse than us.

I have been talking to Mother Nature since childhood and the trees, rocks and animals have always been my friends. I now live on a mountain in British Columbia with my dog, two cats and a worrying amount of chickens.

Somehow I always felt I was destined to become a shaman myself. I consider myself a healer and at home where I have a practice as a physiotherapist I often incorporate dispossession and soul retrieval into my work. All of this finally took form ten years ago when I started taking short courses sponsored by the Foundation of Shamanic Studies. This led on, and I also took a three-year course with them.

After that I took courses in Tibetan, Celtic Sami and Siberian traditions. I wanted to go with Sarangeral to Siberia this summer, but somehow I didn't hear from her for months and gave up on her."

She looked around at us. "You have heard of Sarangerel?" she inquired.

Llyn and I nodded. Sarangeral is a Buryat shaman who was brought up in America. She had written a book that had been well publicized and was called *Riding Windhorses*. This excellent book offered a reading excursion into the ways of Mongolian shamanism.

"Well," Gisela continued, "a friend of mine then told me about this trip with Bill Pfeiffer. I signed up... he didn't. But here I am."

As the stories unraveled so did the string; the next length connected her to Diane.

"Well, I am here because I thought Bill would be on this trip," she started.

"I have long been a supporter of the work done by SEN, but I have never participated in any of their activities up to this time. However, I was drawn to this trip as soon as I learned of it. I experienced a deep desire to come on this journey despite my extreme distrust of airplanes and my nervousness while flying. I am a student of traditional Chinese acupuncture in the Five-Element tradition, but also work part-time as a software engineer to support myself while I am studying."

This short statement concealed Diane's almost pathological fear of flying and she had tapped into a deep well of courage to overcome a real terror as she embarked on this trip, for she had rarely strayed far from the town of her birth.

Then it was my turn and I started to briefly relate how ten years ago the focus of my life had changed dramatically, plunging me onto the path that had led me to this point. But the

Tibetan energies that had been floating all around me now closed in and were too strong to keep under wraps.

The apprehension that I was feeling with these uninvited energies and my confusion as to why they should suddenly be so intrusive bubbled up; and I shared what I was seeing, sharing with these people, who were almost strangers, all of my fears.

There was an instant sense of support, a group bonding and swiftly my anxiety eased. I felt wrapped in a security blanket and started to relax.

I threw the ball of string back to Llyn, making sure I held on to my link. This completed the circle and we all held it taut watching as the smallest tug from one of us reverberated to each member. It was symbolic of our lives, and how any thought or action has an ongoing effect.

"Would someone volunteer to care for this piece of string that has linked us all?" asked Llyn. "We will be taking part in many ceremonies during the next two weeks and I would like whoever takes responsibility for it to ensure that it is with us every time these ceremonies are being performed. The string will naturally absorb the energies drawn in at these gatherings and at the end of our time we will cut it and divide it between us. Each of us will then be taking a special part of this journey back home with us which will help us in our work."

I always chose not to accept any certificate of attendance at the end of any workshop which the majority of people who completed the course and were working in the caring profession were happy to receive. But I recognized the energy that a small piece of string being present in sacred ceremonies would absorb, and knew that this I would treasure.

We followed our verbal sharing by doing what in shamanic terms is called a 'retrieval'. This is achieved by entering a focused form of meditation. In this deeply relaxed state shamans believe you can find the doorway to parallel realities where guiding help is available, help which can be shown in many forms. It can be a word, a person or an object, pretty much anything; however, when the seeker asks the question, "Are you my guide?" the answer will be clear, always a definite yes or no. If it is a no then the quest continues and always something else is shown. Once you receive affirmation of this object you then reach both hands upwards and clasp this invisible object, then holding it tight pull it into your heart, before turning and blowing it into the heart of your partner.

Today Lyn suggested that we do this exercise with a partner and mentally ask for something that would serve as an aid for the forthcoming travels through Siberia.

We paired off and stretched out on the coarse grass, lying close with our sides touching.

Today we were going to retrieve for a partner, so the quest and the question to be asked once the object was visualized was: "Are you the guide for…?" Here we would say their name, then follow the same procedure by reaching up and with cupped hands hold it before blowing it into our partner's heart.

I have participated in this exercise many times and it never ceases to amaze me when someone you have met, in some cases only a very short while previously, will retrieve an object that has a powerful meaning for you.

With instruction from Llyn to change roles from seeker to receiver once the task was completed and to remain in silence until everyone had finished the task and we were all sitting up, we began.

I felt the warm sun on my face and the tension in my muscles slowly slipped away as I relaxed. Llyn watched over us encouraging a soporific state by gently shaking some bead rattles, and within a short space of time we all had our tools.

Mike was given a pyramid.

Diane was given an egg.

Gisela was given a panoramic view of trees with a lake nestling in their middle.

I was given a stone.

These shamanic exercises always have a profound effect on me, and by the time we had divulged and shared the items and visions of each of our journeys I was feeling so much more relaxed and peaceful.

Already it was time for a quick lunch, before we picked up our bags and were on our way back to the airport again.

The final member of our team was waiting for us there, after the hiccup in her flights. We were now complete. I was delighted to recognize her as one of the participants of a week-long DCC workshop that we had both participated in the previous year.

This was Sam, a blond haired lady in her early fifties. We had sat for dinner together several times during that week and I remembered her as a smiling easygoing sort of person.

The knowledge that she was a geologist had stuck in my memory and her career had taken her onto a water-focused path where she spent her time safeguarding our natural water supplies and ensuring that it remained uncontaminated and she always advocated discrimination and care in the use of this precious recourse.

But for the moment all memory of this vanished as my eyes focused on the picture transfer emblazoned across the front of her T-shirt.

It was that of a large grey wolf, identical to the one that had appeared to me so strongly on the flight into Moscow.

We all moved to the departure area and as Sam and I sat next to each other, I took the opportunity to admire it and then ask the question.

"Does it have any special meaning for you?"

"Oh yes," she replied emphatically. "He's one of my spirit guides. In fact at this moment I would say, he's the most important one."

I accepted her response, but refrained from revealing my vision from yesterday.

I find it very reassuring when I attend shamanic workshops, which at this time were very much on the 'fringe' of most people's lives and beliefs, that I am among many people with highly responsible jobs. These people who can balance the awareness of the nonphysical with careers in multinational corporations.

"What has drawn you to this trip?" I asked.

"Well," she started, "seven years ago I was managing multi-million dollar clean-up projects while getting burnt out and feeling lost in the politics of it all. I had always wanted to go to the Andes and I saw this small ad offering a combined trip to the Amazon Rainforest and the Andes Mountains. It was a DCC trip and experiencing the power and influence of one of the most geographically active areas on earth and home to the world's highest active volcano was the uplift I desperately needed. But traveling to their antithesis, the rainforest of the Amazon basin, considered by many to be the lungs of the earth, and to learn from the forest 'masters' gave me the impetus I needed. The indigenous people were an inspiration and my eyes were opened to a new way of thinking."

She smiled at me and her last phrase, "My life changed forever," was one I recognized and resonated with.

She continued, "Traveling with DCC offers such diverse and intense experiences. I was immediately interested in this trip when I first heard about it and that surprised me, since I have never felt drawn to Russia or the surrounding region. It wasn't until many months later and a while after I had put my name forward that quite by accident I learned my father's parents were born in Russia and that my grandfather had served in the Russian Army. It was that information that ignited an immediate burning desire to go.

I was drawn by the stories I then read about how these people integrate their ancestral wisdom and respect for the environment into their daily lives."

"Thank you for sharing that," I said. "I love hearing these stories. Isn't it wonderful how when we listen to our hearts we always end up in the right place?"

The airport was chaotic, but the flight was departing according to the schedule. As we boarded I glanced at Diane; the inside of this Vladivostok airliner had seen better days.

It was filthy and many of the seats were broken and were missing their seat belts, I just hoped they'd spent what few financial resources they obviously had on ensuring the engine and body of this vehicle were sound.

For my companion it was a white-knuckle ride, but the plane took off, flew and landed.

What a relief to arrive in Abakan.

Chapter 3

During the flight to Abakan I started to reread one of John Perkins' books, a small paperback titled Shape Shifting. I had read it previously on my way to Ladakh three years previously and not opened it since, but for some reason I had picked it up again as I prepared my bag for Siberia.

The trip I made to India at that time had confirmed my belief that our lives, to a certain extent, are preordained and that a great network of events conspires to place us in a certain position at a specific time. How we respond and react to the situations or events that unfold is our choice and where our freedom lies.

I never read a book twice and had not touched this one since that time, but before I left home I had been led to bring that one in preference to several unread others.

Already this journey was showing signs that it was going to be special, for on reaching page twenty-seven of this book an amazing synchronicity was revealed.

So many people had been guided to join John on his visits to the Andes and the Amazon, so many workshops and worthy environmental spinoffs had originated from this one man's original dream.

Llyn often assisted John and I was sure this trip was one he would be following closely and I knew without doubt his thoughts and energy would be with us.

This belief appeared to be confirmed as a few pages into his book I read his words about a trip to Mexico he had made many years ago and of his description as he climbed a pyramid at an ancient Mayan site.

In one short paragraph he records the panoramic view from the top and tells of looking out over the treetops, of picking up a stone, and as he looks at it he declares how much it looks like a robin's egg.

Pyramid!

The panoramic view of treetops!

A Stone!

An Egg!

All four of the 'tools' we had retrieved individually for each other just a few hours previously were mentioned in two sentences!

How can one possibly dismiss a connection this extreme by simply giving it the word 'coincidence'?

Moments such as this are signals that something unseen and magical is at work.

Llyn had supervised this ritual, providing the sound of her rattles as we each moved through our journeys, so a tool for her had not been accessed. However, as I reread this one page, I felt my body hairs stand on end. At the top of this pyramid was an object against which John was leaning as he gave this description: a stone jaguar. It was the mention of this stone jaguar that really put the icing on the synchronistic value.

One year previously when our leader had been doing the reconnaissance visit for this trip a shaman had given her the stone medallion of a jaguar. It was the one she had been wearing when she arrived at the airport which was without color or decoration in any way. To some it might have appeared plain, but to me it was beautiful and my eyes were constantly drawn to it.

This was the one she was now still wearing, and when I had earlier commented on it she had told me it was a Tuvan emblem of a coiled panther.

Two names for the same animal; panther is the Old World word for jaguar.

The magic of the synchronicities with our retrieved tools was to continue, but for now I replaced the book in my bag and used the opportunity to have a nap and orient my body to this new time zone.

Before long we were landing in Abakan; as we walked across

the tarmac to the terminal buildings it was still light and surprisingly hot. Who knows what time it was? The correct time was swiftly becoming irrelevant.

There is a luxury in traveling within a group where someone else has made the travel arrangements and has the overall responsibility for getting you to the right place at the right time. I knew it was part of my destiny to be here and I began to relax.

Once again there was an interminable delay in collecting our luggage and once again we had to endure a long single file queue while an official checked the labels and collected our receipts. No one, but no one, escaped this surveillance or passed through the outer doorway without the correct documentation.

We had left Valentina behind in Moscow; now a new interpreter was waiting for us and eager to help in any way she could.

Galena was her name. A slim lady who looked to be in her early forties, smartly dressed and wearing perfect makeup, she would be accompanying us now throughout the rest of our stay.

Finally we had all successfully passed the exit security guards and Galena led us out of the airport doors and into two waiting cars where without further ado we made our way through Abakan and to our hotel.

Again, our stay here would be for one night only, and tomorrow we would be on the move again. The town of Abakan was surprisingly attractive; there were wide tree-lined streets with lots of shops and a bustling appearance as many people of all ages walked along the broad pavements. There was a profusion of young women whose photos would not have looked out of place in a Western fashion magazine; they were tall and blond with a built-in elegance. A multitude of these lithesome young girls were dressed in the latest designer clothes with short skirts and many of them were exhibiting bare midriffs.

It was such a surprise!

The image and expectation I had of Russia in the provinces had been of overweight and dowdy women, with careworn faces and their hair covered by headscarves.

Where were these babushkas? The image that I carried was one I had seen so often presented in our Western press, the propaganda that showed them as the face of Russia. As we walked around I saw a few women such as I had expected but they were certainly in the minority in this part of town.

However, I soon discovered a lot of the younger people were walking around because they were 'promenading'. It is an activity that is free and reminded me of those early photographs of elegant women in their fashionable clothes walking in London's Hyde Park or along the Champs Elysees.

We found our hotel and once more we seemed to be the only guests. Our rooms were again at the end of a long corridor. They were clean but very small and furnished only with a pair of basic single beds holding a very thin mattress, a pillow and a single blanket. A small wooden chest of drawers stood against one wall with a one-foot square mirror hung above it. The provision for hanging up anything was a single hook on the back of the door and the linoleum floor was devoid of even the smallest mat.

The curtains were too small for the windows and fell short on both width and length. Added to this, none of the windows opened and the rooms were airless and stifling.

Contrary to popular belief Siberia is not cold all of the year around and although the temperature in the winter is often 50 degrees below, the point at which the children are allowed a day off school, in June it can get very hot.

I thought my American friends were going to find this very difficult, having been brought up in a country where air conditioning is a fact of life, but there were no complaints and our excitement at being here far outweighed the prospect of some discomfort.

We quickly freshened up and reassembled in the dinning room, a spacious area, but totally soulless and our assumption that we were the only paying occupants seemed confirmed as there was only one table laid up with eight places to accommodate our group.

Potatoes and bread feature highly in the Siberian diet, which is quite understandable given that the land is frozen for eight months of the year. But we weren't here on a gastronomic quest; the meal was edible and filling and the thought of some sleep was more of a priority.

The Tibetan energies that had been so forceful around me earlier in the morning had drifted in and out during the day. They floated rather like a sea mist that envelops a view, then with a mind of its own moves on and vanishes.

This time of the year in this hemisphere the hours of darkness are very short and our room was still full of light when I got into bed, but I was quite exhausted and was sure I would fall into a deep sleep. This was not to be.

Instead, the moment my head touched the pillow... and I am still unsure of whether my physical body fell asleep and remained there or exactly what happened... all I know is that within minutes, I was totally transported to Tibet, a country I have never visited. But for the second time in my life I went via the Amazon Rainforest.

This night in Russia, with my daytime focus on all things Siberian, I totally relived part of a second trip to the Ecuadorian rainforest that I had made in March of the previous year.

One moment I was lying in a hotel bed in a small town in Southern Russia, the next I found myself standing deep in the South American jungle. Although it was nighttime and very dark I somehow knew exactly where I was... It was the small settlement of Miazal, in the rainforests of Ecuador.

I also knew I was about to relive an experience that had terrified me.

This was no dream... I was there!

The constant night sound of the jungle filled my ears, the noise of the river as it flowed past the camp, a sound that I knew continually varied in intensity on an almost hourly basis. The call of myriad nocturnal creatures, the squeaks and whispers of communication between crawling, walking and climbing small animals that inhabited the undergrowth and kept themselves hidden. These sounds were accompanied by the creaking of the trees and the fluttering down of a dinner plate-sized dry leaf.

All of this along with the distinctive smell of the jungle surrounded me but the overriding sound was none of these.

It was one that was totally out of place... I was hearing chanting. It was the deep sound of a group of monks chanting. Then I heard the gong of brass being struck; it rang loud and clear.

At this point I became aware of a man standing silently next to me. It was John. This man who was my mentor and who had spent many years living and working with the Shuar people before bringing small groups of Westerners into this remote area to observe how these fierce headhunters were also the most gentle, loving people.

This is a tribe that lived their lives with great care and respect for our planet and everything that dwelt on it, a way of life that so many of us need to relearn.

In an inexplicable and mysterious way I had been transported from my bed in Siberia to revisit and relive an experience that had occurred 18 months ago.

The sound of the chanting penetrated my very being. I felt it vibrating through me and I said to John, "The chanting! The monks!"

Where was it all coming from?

I heard my companion say just three words: "Go with it."

Instantly both he and the jungle vanished along with all of its sounds and smells.

It was no longer dark. I found myself in broad daylight and moving across a large square, cobbled courtyard. It was the central area of a temple complex, a Buddhist temple in Tibet. This was something I just knew without question.

This was where I was.

The fact that I have never been to that country was immaterial. There was not a shadow of doubt that this building was in this land.

It was extraordinary, somehow I was still me but at the same time everything about me had changed.

I was male!

I was a monk wearing a saffron-colored robe which flapped against my legs as I walked. A glance down revealed the sandals on my feet which were no more than a couple of thick dusty leather straps.

This was so strange.

As Wendy and the persona I embody in this lifetime, it was footwear I wouldn't touch. But in this fleeting moment, there came a sense of recognition and comfort in seeing these well worn items clinging to my feet.

The sound of the chanting was getting louder. It was coming from a building to the right of me and I knew that was where I was heading. But without changing my pace I continued going straight forward for somehow I knew that to access this area I needed to walk the way I was going.

I had the sense that I was late and there was an urgency in my steps. There was also a sense of familiarity, an understanding that I was about to perform a task that I had been trained for, a unique and demanding role, but one that I had accepted and embraced without question.

The exterior of the buildings that surrounded me were colored in rich reds, blues and golds, and had decorative trimmings. A few shallow steps ran the length of the building I was headed for, and above it was a long-pillared portico to walk under before entering the building proper.

But I didn't get that far.

A feeling of fear suddenly washed over me. I stopped in my

tracks as a blanket of absolute terror descended on me.

I knew I was about to face something indescribably horrendous and I could go no further.

The scene at that moment disappeared and I felt myself falling... falling down into darkness.

Then with my heart still pounding I found I was once more in the jungle, standing only a few yards from the round room, the area where my companions and the shamans were participating in an ayahuasca ceremony.

My physical body did not appear to have left this place. John was still standing there next to me and I heard him say, "Wendy. Would you prefer to go and sit down?"

This man's long shamanic training and his natural instincts pick up emotions as surely as if he had visible antennae. I was not aware that I had said anything and whatever my facial expression had divulged it was non-revealing for the night was very dark.

"I am scared," I stated. "Soooo scared," and I fought to keep back the tears.

Then the chanting started again. It was like a magnet, calling me back, sucking me in and the fear swept over me again.

"NO!" I shouted. "I can't go. I CAN'T!"

John was very calm. "Just take your time," I heard him say.

I felt myself almost physically moving out of the jungle, being drawn elsewhere; and much as I resisted it, the pull was too strong.

"They're calling me. Can't you hear them? You must hear it," I demanded.

John is always supportive, but in his wisdom knows that we each have our own path to walk and at the end of the day we are the ones who have to handle whatever life presents us with.

Whether he saw what I was seeing or heard what I was hearing, he didn't say. He knew it was my journey and my learning process

"Just face it," he said. "See what it holds for you."

Somewhere in my deepest subconscious I knew I had to go forward. To not do so would, I knew, have left me with the deepest regrets. Whatever was about to happen was something I had to face and conquer.

I surrendered to the call of the chanting, feeling myself being drawn back into the incarnation of a Tibetan monk. Once again I was hurrying across the stone courtyard.

The fear hit me like a sledgehammer and I fought to hold drown the screams that were trying to burst from my throat.

I stopped.

Then somehow I summoned up the courage to continue and almost dragging one foot at a time to place it in front of the other I reached the portico, went up the three shallow steps and walked a few steps to the right where I found myself outside of a closed door.

This was the room where the sound of male voices chanting was emitting.

I placed my hand on the handle of the door. I knew that within a short time of entering it I would be witness to a future event of unimaginable horrors. My heart was pounding and it felt as if my head was about to explode, but I knew I had no choice but to go forward to open the door and step in.

I turned the handle...

At that precise moment it all vanished.

The scene. The fear. All emotion and energy relating to this experience just disappeared in a trice.

I woke up and opened my eyes. The room was in a half-light and for a moment I felt very disorientated.

Then I realized I was in a hotel in Siberia!

Why now had this experience from several years ago been resurrected as I started off on this journey to Tuva?

I had recorded it in my journal at the time, but then moved on... my life was full of other things and it was not a memory I had dwelt on.

It made no sense.

But I was so exhausted that I must have immediately fallen back into sleep for the next thing I knew I was waking up after having passed the rest of the night in a dreamless state. It was now Monday morning. Some very strange things were happening.

It was all so bizarre.

Although Siberia is now part of the Russian Federation, the very word still evokes visions of a country that is quite unique. Its sheer size makes it awesome. More than six thousand miles across, its land mass occupies one third of the Northern Hemisphere and to travel from one side to the other you must pass through seven time zones. These are statistics on a grand scale.

Cares regarding our families and occupations had by now vanished. This was before the days of cell phones. We would be totally out of touch, and there was an indulgent feeling of living in the moment and the moment belonged totally to us.

Today we would be traveling by road, viewing close up a small portion of this vast country. We were in high spirits at breakfast and starting to bond as a group and all buzzing with excitement.

As Sam had missed the retrieval exercise, Llyn asked me if I would journey for her and do the retrieval and we did indeed find five minutes space in the midst of a busy day to engage in this small ritual and again I held the Universe in awe at the confirmation that the rightful tool was retrieved for her.

The ritual was done as we lay on the cold linoleum covered floor of a hotel bedroom in Siberia, so very far away from anything that would give a clue as to the gift that would be offered.

We lay down side by side on this hard cold floor and no sooner had I closed my eyes than I felt a huge mental shift as I found myself with a small group of American Native Indians in a time that I instinctively knew was many years ago.

It was nighttime and very cold and I was clutching a blanket that was wrapped around me, although it was dark I knew a vast open space extended beyond us. I sat with a small group of others around an open and small but brightly burning fire.

I bent forward and brushed away some of the sand in front of me and picked up an object. As I looked at it I saw it was a small but thick arrowhead.

Almost before I had completed the act of asking the question, "Is this Sam's tool?" I knew the answer would be *yes*.

I retrieved the mental image of the gift and blew it into Sam's heart.

The exercise had been completed so quickly and as we sat up there was some reservation on my companion's face as I prepared to tell her what gift had been given.

"It's an Indian arrowhead," I said.

As the words came out of my mouth I saw her jaw drop and her eyes welled up. Then she shared with me the fact that recently she and her husband had felt drawn to purchase a piece of land in Arizona, a large plot that they had felt a great affinity with, although it would be many years before they could afford to build a house. They spent as much time as possible wandering across it and sitting dreaming of the time when they could be there permanently.

They discovered that this land had, at one time, belonged to the Anzani Indians, and the pair of them were continually searching for anything that had once belonged to these people and had remained hidden and undisturbed on the land.

Further confirmation that this was indisputably Sam's tool from the spirits would come later.

Llyn had been busy doing a deal with our transport and somehow she had negotiated the exchange of our planned transport, which was a small people carrier, with that of a twenty-seater coach.

This coach had apparently been originally earmarked for a group of Japanese men, but we blessed her persuasive powers for it would be a very long journey and the weather was getting very hot. Now there would be so much more room for us, plus we could carry a relief driver.

With her foresight we were reaping the rewards of the testing experiences she had met with on her earlier recce visits. And while she finalized our ongoing plans with Galena, her words "Be as quick as you can!" ringing in our ears, the rest of us set out for the shops to purchase a few requirements for the journey ahead.

Like most of the objects in this country the vehicle to take us on this long journey conformed by being clean but ancient and we piled the back seats with our entire luggage; two of the other seats were requisitioned for bottles of water and food for the long journey ahead.

We had bread, cheese, bananas and biscuits and in our joyful state that looked like a feast. We'd purchased flowers and some colored ribbons to decorate the interior of the bus and as we set off our ears were filled with the driver's choice of music playing loudly.

To the outside world we probably looked like a group of gypsies!

Our destination was the small country of Tuva and the town of Kyzyl.

Within a few miles we began to appreciate the space we had as the temperature outside soared and inside the coach it also began to climb rapidly. This vehicle had certainly been built before air conditioning had come along. There also appeared to be no vents to let the heat of the engine escape and we all became acutely aware of some dubious fumes that started to flow.

Behind the driver was a seat that faced the rear and this is where I started off but very soon it was like being wrapped in a heated electric blanket with a broken thermostat. We were just an hour into our journey and I was about to move to another seat when we came to a halt, our first stop initiated by a need for the engine to cool down. This was to be the pattern for the rest of the day and into the evening as we continued our long journey.

But it was no problem. We were on shamanic time, we all accepted we were exactly where we were supposed to be and there was no pressure on the timekeeping for Llyn had no meetings organized until the following day.

There was almost no traffic on the road, just the odd car or two going in the opposite direction and we passed through no towns. Occasionally there would be a hamlet of wooden single-story buildings, each set in its own small fenced-in patch.

Cows wandered freely across the road in these small pockets of habitation, but rarely was there a sighting of either man, woman or child.

The landscape was much wooded but interspersed with large stretches of grassland; the green was patched with yellow and white signaling a profusion of wild flowers. These open areas stretched way into the distance, were unfenced and totally devoid of cattle and habitation.

Every hour or so we had an enforced stop to allow the engine to cool and we would all emerge from the bus to get out, stretch our legs and breathe in the fume-free air.

On one of these stops we were suddenly surrounded by butterflies; thousands upon thousands of them engulfed us. They were all white with black spots, the Dalmatian of the butterfly world, but they seemed to have come to this particular place to die, for the ground around us was a carpet of black and white dying or dead insects.

We climbed back onto the bus and continued our journey and for several miles this same species of butterflies were crashing into the coach or being sucked into the air flow and ending up inside.

It was a very strange phenomenon. The sheer volume of these small insects was astounding; rather like salmon: once they have made the long return route to where they spawned they too die. Our interpreter told us this was a yearly event and they always congregated en masse in this same place to end their short lifespan.

There was a fun mood prevailing in our bus, lots of laughter and excitement and before too long we reached the base of the Sayan Mountains and here the road began to climb. The bus struggled as we went around and up, then around and down with the view from our mobile base stretching further by the minute.

At one point as we passed between two peaks we stopped and alighted and here we performed an ancient ritual. Lyn had come this way on her previous visit to Tuva and showed us the local way of honoring the spirits of the mountain.

Perched high on the side with an unguarded edge that dropped thousands of feet we sprinkled milk and scattered bread and echoed Llyn as she shouted to the unseen guardians, "Take it! Take it!"

We made our offerings to all the spirits of the heavens and the earth, to the guardians of the four directions and to the mountain that our feet rested on.

This is an ancient ceremony asking for a safe passage as we traveled, and away in the distance we heard a rumble of thunder, the voice of the dragon and we hoped it was a sign from the gods giving their blessing.

We made several other brief stops when we parked at the side of the road next to an ovaa, which is a structure that marks the site of a sacred place.

To the uninitiated this would like just like a heap of stones but distinguishing it from this were the decorative attachments. A supported post stood in the middle, and tied to the top of this were lengths of string that spread out to the extreme edges of the base where they were secured by a large rock.

Numerous strips of different-colored pieces of rag were tied along each piece of string, all of it faded and frayed by the constant flapping in the wind.

From Galena and Llyn we came to understand the importance the local people attach to these sites and how they attach horse hair and cloths as a physical representation of their prayers and hopes...

By marking their wishes in these scared spots they hoped that the power would be granted to manifest their intentions for these ovaas represent the union between the three worlds, between all places and all times and thus they have great shamanic power.

Again under Llyn's guidance and with not too much searching we each found a large rock and individually we placed it on top of the existing stones thus adding our token to honor the spirits and pray for a safe passage.

As I added mine I noticed several small coins had been reverently placed at some time in the past and also a few un-smoked cigarettes were tucked down in the gaps.

As the road had climbed ever higher we began to pass through areas where these mountaintops were white capped. Occasionally we would pass a large mound of still-frozen snow on the roadside where the sun had failed to touch it. Snow disguised with a dirty grey coat from the fumes of exhausts from vehicles such as ours.

The outside temperature was now quite low but the heat inside our coach was almost unbearable and the chocolate bars we had purchased were swimming in the bag. However, it seemed nothing could deflate our high spirits and as we reached the checkpoint into the province of Tuva not even the somber expressions of the guards and the unnecessary delay they imposed dented our mood.

As we descended from the mountainous area, the outside air temperature started to rise, and finally, hot, dusty and tired we arrived in Kyzyl.

Our hotel stood on a road opposite what were the KGB headquarters. This is an older, attractive-looking building from the outside and we were not surprised when we later discovered that it was one of the few structures in the town that was in good repair.

Pleasingly, all of our bedrooms were to the rear of the hotel and overlooked the river. The Yenisei at this point is wide and fast flowing, and as we gazed across its expanse to the other side the land seemed to disappear into infinity. It was just scrubland, treeless tundra disappearing into the far distant mountains.

During this daylong trek, the noise from the engine of our bus meant we had to shout to communicate so it had made general conversation quite difficult. I had spent much of the journey simply with my thoughts and focusing on the passing landscape. Thankfully, even in this slightly meditative state there had been no untoward intrusion and all Tibetan thoughts and energies had remained absent.

Now although it was late evening it was still light, for June in Siberia is called the time of the White Nights and there is only darkness between about 11.00 pm and 4.00 am.

However, we were all tired and rather than explore our surroundings we opted for bed and an early breakfast.

I must have fallen asleep almost as soon as my head hit the pillow and once more during the night a Tibetan influence prevailed. This time it was a dream, but a dream with great clarity that remained when I awoke many hours later and which I found hard to decipher.

I was standing in MOMA, the famous art museum in New York, when a Buddhist monk walked past and beckoned me to follow him. He walked along a corridor and opened a door. I moved along behind him and once through the door it closed behind us. There was a cinema screen at one end of the room and just one chair placed in the center of this room facing the screen.

He indicated for me to sit on it and as I did so a large painting of a Tibetan tapestry appeared on the screen; the monk then disappeared. I sat for several minutes just staring at this picture, then that too disappeared, and as soon as it did all recall of what it held vanished and I could remember no specific detail or image on it.

A strange dream, but the mystery continued, for at breakfast the following morning, when we were all sitting at a round table, Llyn asked, "Does anyone want to share his or her dreams?"

I replied by saying, "You go first."

She followed this by describing how she found herself standing in front of a blank wall when suddenly there appeared on it the images of two identical Tibetan tapestries. When I followed her by telling my dream, she shared my amazement, but it left us puzzled for neither of us had any comprehension of the meaning.

Chapter 4

Tuva is known as the Land of the Female Shaman and there was one shaman in particular that we were anxious to meet.

Her name is Ai-Churek, but she was more often referred to as Moon Heart. Llyn had been able to meet her on Llyn's earlier visit to this land and had sent us each a brief biography of this remarkable woman to read before we embarked on our journey.

The plan was that we would travel to her homeland, deep in the heart of Tuva, and this was what Llyn had put much time and effort into arranging. Now at breakfast she reminded us of a few meaningful details of the life of this remarkable woman.

"I am sure you were all overwhelmed by the story of Moon Heart," she commenced. "Last time I was here one of the other shamans told me she can create rain from a clear blue sky."

We all looked closely at Llyn, wanting to believe and hoping we would have the opportunity to witness such a powerful event.

She continued, "I know the last couple of days have been very tiring, but let's put them behind us now and focus on what is ahead. We will be meeting her later today so try to center yourselves as you prepare to enter multidimensional realities.

I know this will be a powerful time and I feel it would help if we reminded ourselves of her story."

At that point our interpreter arrived accompanied by another Russian lady who she introduced as Rollanda Kongar.

Rollanda spoke perfect English without a trace of an accent. Most of her time we learned was spent teaching at the Kyzyl High School and her appearance was that of the picture book schoolmarm with a severe tied-back hairstyle and black-rimmed glasses. Now during the school holidays she was supplementing her income by acting as an interpreter. She would, we learned, be assisting Galena and they would both be caring for us throughout our stay in Tuva.

After the introductions were complete Llyn said, "We were just reminding ourselves of Moon Heart's history. Perhaps you could tell us her story, Rollanda? I am sure there is a lot you can share with us."

Rollanda had had a close affiliation with the Tuva Shamans and for many years she had been working as an unpaid assistant to a man named Mongush Kenin Lopsan, who is the curator of the Museum of Shamanism in Tuva and a writer of the history of the Siberian shaman.

With a reply of "Yes. Certainly," Rollanda took up the story.

"Ai-Churek's father was a horse thief and her mother was born into the Kara deeger uktuch kham people, who are celestial shamans. On the night of her birth there was a violent thunderstorm, but the legend goes that the moment this baby let out her first cry the rains ceased, the wind died down and the moon appeared. Because her father was used to spending entire nights in the forest and was accustomed to the elements, he saw this as a divine sign and chose for his child the name of Moon Heart.

Early in her life Moon Heart's mother died and she was sent to live with relatives who did not understand her when she played with the spirits and ran with the wind. They punished her for these actions, but Moon Heart secretly continued to celebrate ancient traditions and her gifts started to manifest.

At this time the Soviet Union had erected atheism as a state 'religion' and persecuted those that did not comply. Moon Heart's relatives were frightened by her behavior and their fear of the authorities so when they failed to control and stop her actions they placed her into a mental institution. From there she was sent to Moscow to study electrical engineering. She stayed in the capital for nine years but she realized she had inherited her mother's gifts and when Perestroika arrived she returned to Tuva.

Here she was free to travel out to the Taiga where in complete solitude she could contact the forces of Nature and develop her shamanic gifts.

In 1991 she met Kenin Lopsan, who recognized her talents and invited her to work in the shamanic clinic, the Tungar Clinic in Kyzyl, where she now works as a shaman healing people with the use of herbs and by calling on the assistance of unseen spirits and guides."

We sat like children transfixed by the story as Rollanda's words entranced us and we wanted to hear more.

She continued, "Moon Heart works with the stars, especially the constellation of the Great Bear. She addresses herself to the stars. She says they help her to see the weakness and the force of a person, his disease and his talents. She invokes the star of the sick person and if the star almost falls she knows the person will be healed.

With the use of the sound from the khoomei horn and the drum she enters an altered state of consciousness and contact with the spirits happens mentally.

Music has a magical force which the spirits of the mountains love."

I was beginning to understand why I was here. There was a force propelling my life that outweighed all resistance. The strength of it swept me along submerging all of my desire to be a stay at home grandmother, safe in the bosom of my family in England.

"Kenin Lopsan has agreed to give a lecture just for you this morning. His talk will be very special, because it is based on a subject he has not spoken about in public before."

She looked around at all of us and gave a brief smile as she recognized we were all suitably impressed.

She continued by telling us more about this now elderly gentleman, a man who has devoted his life to the study of mysticism and is a recognized authority on shamanism. She has spent many hours writing and recording his great knowledge and told how he endorses an academic approach to this subject and is much respected by the Tuvan people.

Now with travel into Tuva becoming less difficult, his fame is rapidly spreading as yearly more visitors arrive from distant lands and listen attentively to his lectures. In the twilight of his life his great knowledge is beginning to be shared.

Siberia is the home of shamanism and shamanism is the mother religion (as I said, it is where the very word originated) and Tuva, this small country within the boundaries of Siberia, is famed for the power of its shamans.

Here we were not only in the center of Asia but the epicenter of this immense unseen power.

We prepared ourselves for an exciting day.

Our first visit today was to be to the Kyzyl Museum to visit the professor. This is the title by which Kenin Lopsan is referred; whether it is a diploma held title or an honorary one is irrelevant for he has certainly earned the right to be so addressed.

The day was already very hot and it was mid-morning by the time we set off. We walked trying to keep in any shade we could find. From our hotel we passed dreary tenement buildings which at first seemed empty. They were grey and bleak and devoid of any children playing in the area and appeared to be empty, but signs of clothes washing strung up changed the belief of our first impression.

The washing hung limp and grey, a sign that soap or detergents were products either difficult to purchase or the cost was prohibitive.

All around us was continuous evidence that life was hard in this place; silently we absorbed this information, a reminder to be thankful for all the things in our daily lives that we take so much for granted.

The museum is housed in a large wooden, single-story building. A beautiful old structure but one that gives the curator a constant headache as he daily views this fire hazard that contains so many irreplaceable treasures.

To one side of this main building, with just a dirt yard separating them, was another single-story wooden building but much smaller. This looked little more than a shed with just a door and one window, but it housed two rooms, one of which was the professor's office. We stepped into what looked like a storeroom stacked high with cardboard boxes and Rollanda went though another door to see if the master was ready. She was back in a few moments and we then all filed into another tiny and equally filled room.

This was to be a private lecture. We were privileged in that he was prepared to share some of his unseen written papers with us, papers that he had not used in any previous lecture and Rollanda would translate his words for us.

The gentleman himself was standing behind his desk waiting to greet us; he stood upright in regal pose and looked magnificent.

A large man, his image was in great contrast to his bleak surroundings. He had a profusion of white hair and his full-length gown was of an emerald green color and the heavy satin material was richly embroidered with gold thread.

On his desk, among a mountain of papers, sat the matching hat that would have completed the regalia, but the temperature in this confined space must have been in the nineties and the man was breathing heavily and sweating profusely.

He had obviously made enormous effort to present himself as the respected shaman held in high esteem by the populace of this town.

To this group from the West he was representing Tuvan shamanism. He did it justice; our eyes beheld a powerful image. Through Rollanda he warmly welcomed us, and then gave a deep groan as he eased himself down into his chair.

Next Rollanda busied herself moving in an assortment of old chairs and stools for us to sit on and once we were comfortably settled there was a pregnant silent pause. It was pure theatre as with a great flourish of the sleeves of his robe Kenin Lopsan began to talk.

His lecture was entitled "The Counts of Mysterious Language" and he held us spellbound as his discourse covered the long-held belief that every single thing that happens eventually intersects with each of our lives; nothing happens by chance.

He spoke of his belief that there is a great universal plan, a cosmic arrangement in which we humans play a small part, but equally the movement of every living creature on this planet has a meaning and a role.

He covered so many subjects and in great detail, even claiming that the meaning when a bird flew across in front of us offered a different message if it flew from the right or the left.

For me it was when he spoke about horses that his words made a very strong impact and I listened closely as I heard these words, while Rollanda kept up a speedy translation.

"If a horse refuses to cross a ford or walk through a stream, it is because there are bad water spirits about. The horse with his sensitivity will adhere to the demands of these spirits."

My mind instantly flashed back to an incident that had happened several years ago.

I had been out on my horse and was returning home. This horse I had purchased as a six-month-old foal over eight years ago and at three years old I had started riding him. His stable was outside my backdoor and we went out along the bridle path and into the countryside most days. We spent many hours together and he was an animal with whom I had a great affinity.

On this particular day our route led us across a small ford. This was one we had passed through on numerous occasions without incident. But today as we reached the water, which at that time was no more than a foot deep, gently flowing as it usually was and stretched to about fifteen feet, my horse stopped dead. Normally he walked through without breaking his stride, but today he dug in his toes and flatly refused to put a hoof into the water.

There was nothing visible to alarm him and I tried all manner of persuasion without success.

It was infuriating because I was only fifteen minutes from home and to retrace our steps would have taken nearly an hour.

I tried coaxing, cajoling, I even dismounted prepared to get my feet soaking wet and tried to lead him across, all to no avail. The need to return home by the shortest route was a necessity for I happened to be on the school run that day and had children waiting to be collected.

After some fifteen minutes of stubbornly refusing to cross this small piece of water, of even rearing up and standing on his back legs to enforce his feelings, there was a subtle shift.

The sun continued to shine and there had been no wind, but something changed in the air around us, a tangible movement in the energies and I observed a relaxation of my horse's attitude.

From an adamant refusal he suddenly put one leg forward and walked firmly across, splashing through the water as he had always done.

The visual picture of this particular day had always remained with me and as the professor spoke of the water spirits it triggered the memory and I happily settled with his words as an explanation of my horse's behavior.

Kenin Lopsan finally brought his lecture to a close; our attention had been held so raptly that we had been oblivious to the heat of the room and the discomfort of the hard chairs. After answering a few questions Rollanda sensed that this great man was tiring and firmly brought the meeting to a close. She produced a beer for him and he generously indicated for her to offer one to each of us.

Before we left he asked for all of our dates of birth, and taking a piece of paper that already had our names on he wrote this information alongside.

We expressed our thanks and gratitude and with our heads feeling like overloaded sponges and leaving our interpreter to fuss over him, Galena led the rest of us out into the brilliant and hot sunshine.

We paused before crossing the dirt yard towards the museum and we gathered in a group voicing our admiration for this man.

He had spoken with such wisdom and shared a little of his vast accumulation of knowledge in a simplistic fashion expressing his desire that the information he possessed be of benefit to all.

As we stood there together, an incident occurred to cement our memories of this moment.

From out of the sky an eagle swooped down coming almost into the yard. Clearly we could see his eye; he skimmed over the professor's office and circled over the roof of the museum seeming to salute us. Then with a flap of his large wings, he rose back up and disappeared back into the sky to continue his journey.

For this part of the country seeing an eagle is probably not a rare occurrence, but for us the sight of this magnificent bird at close quarters with all his freedom was very special.

By the time we had made the few steps that took us into the museum Rollanda had caught up with us and liaised as the assistant curator introduced herself. We were invited to wander freely through the four rooms which led one into the other and to request assistance for information if and when we desired it.

Her offer was accepted and with Galena also on hand to translate we strolled around, being the only visitors at present and we spread out, each of us drawn to different items.

As I entered the second room I saw Mike, Sam and Jennifer were already engrossed in some items in a glass cabinet that was hanging on one of the walls, and as I joined them the assistant curator had just finished talking and Rollanda began her interpretation. I looked at the item to which she was referring and felt a strange sense of déjà vu.

It was the large original medallion from which Llyn's soapstone copy had been made.

This item grabbed at me. It was so familiar, it was like looking at a favorite piece of my own jewelry and I felt it pull on my heartstrings.

The item at which we were all gazing and receiving information about was a large piece of bronze with the most intricate detail. It depicted the coiled panther. I heard the words: "Almost identical pieces of this item crafted in both gold and silver are on display in Russia's largest museum that is in Moscow.

This brooch was the insignia of the famous women warriors of Tuva. The coiled panther was worn only by the bravest of the brave."

The others moved on to view more articles and I remained totally transfixed by this item and was unaware as they then left the room while I remained there gazing at it.

I stood there alone in this dusty, dimly-lit room surrounded by ancient sacred shamanic artifacts with this coiled panther object seeming to have a magnetic hold on me, and into my head came snatches of memory that, like pieces of a jigsaw, started to float before my eyes.

The forgotten memory of a stay deep in the Amazon Rainforest and a Shuar shaman telling me I was a great warrior returned.

Where had this come from?

Throughout my life any strange and extraordinary 'coincidences' have finally enforced a belief in reincarnation. In the middle of a regular ordinary day something would happen that would stop me in my tracks and promulgate this unprovable idea.

In that moment I knew there were also other things to be recalled which remained for the present tantalizingly just out of reach and I knew I had to be patient.

Finally I refocused on the present and reluctantly turned my back on this glass case and moved on into a further connecting room. Here the articles on display were sparse and, as in the previous rooms, all safely in glass cabinets which either stood against or hung from the walls.

They were easy to view for they were spaced out, the quantity was meager and I was also the only one present in this area.

A few paces in and my jaw dropped. I couldn't believe what I was seeing.

This was also so unexpected!

There before my eyes was a wooden carving, a large mask with the decorative paintwork still in good condition and bright with color.

The image I was looking at was the head of a Tibetan deity.

It was a blood-red color, with fanged teeth. The eyes were large and bulbous and adorning the head was a band of skulls carved in miniature. This was a material representation of the god that I carried in my head.

The Maha Kala, a power revered by the Tibetans.

How could this be?

The essence and force of this deity had first encompassed me on a trip to Ladakh three years ago when I had felt the power of him enter me.

This image that I had first felt in the vastness of the Himalayan Mountains, that I had again encountered in the Amazon Rainforest and the same one that had penetrated my sleep two nights ago, here in Siberia.

What was happening?

What did it mean?

What was the connection that so powerfully linked me to this ancient deity?

Nothing in this lifetime had prepared me for this. I had no particular interest in Buddhism. I had never been drawn to read any books on this dogma.

The Tibetans respect and pay homage to many, many deities. The image depicted here I would later learn goes under many names and as well as Maha Kala he is also called Yama, the god of death and destruction, but also referred to as the White Protector.

What a mystical and sacred realm surrounds us. But for most of us who live a traditional Western life reveling in the materiality of it all, this unseen world passes us by, escaping our notice.

Here I was, now a grandmother who until a few years ago was a corporate wife fully embracing the lifestyle that accompanied this position and enjoying all of the material benefits and at that time had no thought of or desire to search for the mystical side of life.

The dramatic events that unfolded in 1990 changed these views and propelled me on a quest, the start of what the learned Joseph Campbell calls, "The Hero's Journey".

My participation on this trip to Siberia was part of a never-ending search, but I had no idea what I was on the brink of at this moment and the Tibetan energies now surrounding me were puzzling and mystifying.

Maybe a lot of the time it is not necessary to know why these things happen and for some these unusual circumstances would be ignored or dismissed, but for me they provoke a deep desire for understanding. It feeds my need to learn more of our unseen world.

I wandered through the rest of the museum under the pretense of looking but was oblivious now to all before me, and as we returned to the hotel I walked alongside my companions on the sunbaked pavements with them physically but alone in my thoughts.

The sense that I was on the brink of something extraordinary prevailed and it left me feeling apprehensive.

At lunch Llyn verbally gave us the itinerary for the rest of the day and advised us to use the half hour before we embarked on this program to take a brief nap.

I lay on my bed, but it was impossible to sleep. My head was filled with the Tibetan connections and energies that had swamped me since we left New York.

Questions without answers spun round and round in my head.

I was trying to do the impossible and make some sense of the inexplicable.

It required more than a little effort to move from the bed, but much lay ahead to look forward to. This afternoon we were to meet the Tuvan shamans and among them would be the renowned Moon Heart.

The lady had just returned from Italy where she had been sponsored to do workshops and seminars. Her large following there have been witness to the performance of many powerful ceremonies. Now her ability and fame were beginning to spread throughout Europe and into America.

We set off with Rollanda and Galena walking in front and leading the way along a path that ran alongside the river. This path would no doubt one day be transformed into a paved promenade, but for the present it was a rough tarmac footpath, in need of repair with many potholes that needed avoiding.

Here we were on the eastern side of the Yenisei. This river starts near the Mongolian border and divides Siberia as it ploughs its way to the Arctic Ocean.

It was difficult to equate this fact to the mid-afternoon temperature that now reached well over eighty degrees. This heat was totally unexpected and very tiring.

Added to this was a problem we were totally unused to... a plague of mosquitoes. Swarms of them and there was no escaping the incessant buzzing around our heads and continuous bites. They seemed to find us a delicacy and the word was out!!

After a ten-minute walk along this tree-lined path, we saw

ahead of us an untidy collection of small single-storied wooden buildings that on closer inspection would prove to be interconnecting.

We saw that there were also two yurts set up, the traditional round Siberian dwellings still used by the nomadic people, and these had been erected between the buildings and the bank of the river.

This site, we would learn, was the base for the organization of the Tuvan shamans known as "Tos Deer" (Nine Heavens), of which Ai-Churek was the head. Small groups of people were milling in front and as we drew nearer all heads turned towards us as we approached.

We were a motley group, very diverse from the Tuvan physical uniformity, for ninety percent of Tuvans have jet-black hair and their height seems to fall into the six-inch range between five feet and five feet six inches.

There was an extreme physical range within our group. Diane is a fraction over five feet tall and Mike who is representative of all good things American is well built and almost six foot, four inches in height. While Gisela is also a tall woman, but model slim, and the other four of us had varying heights and shapes in between.

Not only were we to later find that those in more isolated regions found the difference in our heights interesting, it would also be our skin tones and the color of our hair that drew their attention.

Llyn's hair is auburn, long, thick and explosive with lots of curl; Jennifer's dark hair now sported this Rastafarian style, while mine is straight, blond and very long.

Physically we were all very different.

As we arrived and stopped in front of the first yurt, the chatter of the onlookers ceased, as without guile they looked us up and down. Then they parted as a male shaman moved through the small crowd and approached us.

With the coming of Perestroika came rumors of shamans surviving in remote areas, but this went uncorroborated for several years.

The rumors proved true and here was our proof.

This shaman, a slim-built man who looked to be in his forties, was wearing black trousers under a long black tunic, with a waistcoat of this same base color trimmed with animal fur. The tunic had eight or nine metal rods stitched to it and the bottom edge was fringed with strips of rainbow-colored ribbons.

Around his neck hung several small reflective round discs, the tool the shaman uses to aid in his talent for scrying, the art of seeing into the future.

Completing his outfit was a feathered headdress. The feathers were all shades of cream and brown color, probably from an eagle, and this extended down the length of his back.

Gathered behind him were two older women. They too were wearing brightly-colored shamanic robes with ornate embroidery. These also had many feathers hanging from their voluminous skirts, which were also trimmed with colored ribbons along the hem. Both of them had numerous rings, bracelets and necklaces which clinked as they moved.

At this time it was ten years after the fall of the collectivist ideology and the few remaining shamans who had survived were now free to follow their beliefs and to wear their treasured traditional shamans' robes.

In the early 1930s, it was estimated that Tuva had 1,000 shamans, but the advent of Communism announced the death of all relative beliefs. Atheism prevailed and shamans who continued to practice these ancient rituals were persecuted and shot. Ceremonial robes, the many beautiful feathered headdresses, the drums and flails were destroyed and burnt. All that remained were the few rescued remnants that were now on show in the Kyzyl Museum and what, under pain of death, had been kept hidden for years and I was now seeing.

One of the shaman's many roles is as the keeper of his people's memory of stories and traditions that are the foundation of this culture. He has his own inherited secrets, the ability to enter a trance state where he meets with the ancestral spirits seeking help and guidance for the well-being of his community. He holds the power to either recruit or repulse these spirits and in secret places he would invoke his animal spirit guides.

Those brave people who continued to keep alive these ancient traditions did so at severe risk of losing their lives and of necessity went 'underground'.

Rollanda stepped forward to meet the shamans, they conversed briefly in Russian, and then turning to us she said: "You have been invited into this yurt," and she indicated to the one on the right. "Please remove your shoes and then go in and make yourself comfortable."

Even the smallest of us had to bend low to enter its small doorway, and after the brightness of the sunshine at first it seemed a little dark, but it was cool and a relief to be out of the heat and away from the interminable buzz and bites of the mosquitoes.

The design and build of these mobile homes have remained unchanged over the centuries. They are round and the two on this site both had a diameter of about twenty feet. The side stands up to about four feet, and then the wooden strutted roof reaches from this level to a peaked dome which has a small circular opening.

The structure is covered with heavy felt and the hinged wood door can seal the entrance. The floor, apart from a small area in the center, was covered in heavy rugs, many of them ornately woven with bright red and blue threads.

Always in the center of yurts in use and standing directly on the ground will be a potbellied stove. Fuelled only by wood they provide the heat, and we were soon to discover with amazing ingenuity the cook will daily produce from this one source large nourishing meals to feed the family.

Today several families will share the costs and use an open-back truck to load the yurt onto and travel in, thus allowing them to follow their animals as they graze the open plains in the summer months. This means that they can now carry a little more furniture than would have been possible in the past. Now there is often one or two iron-framed beds and a chest or cupboard to provide some furnishings.

At the back, opposite the entrance door was a long low cupboard with a distinctly Chinese appearance, again painted in the reds and blues. It depicted a flame-breathing dragon. On one side of this yurt was a long seat that would double as a bed, the obligatory stove sat in the center and the floor felt soft to the feet as there were several layers of horsehair matting under the showpiece top carpets, and around the rest of the inside perimeter were many assorted cushions.

We each found a cushion and with Galena to answer any questions we seated ourselves on the floor. As I gazed upwards I saw the blue sky through the central hole and as the sunshine pierced this aperture the wooden struts supporting the roof splayed out as if they were rays from the sun.

How wonderful it must look I thought when the sun reached its zenith and the joy of lying in bed on a clear night with an uninterrupted view of the stars.

Once more an intense feeling of déjà vu swept over me and I knew I was touching on a past life as my heart started to ache, my eyes filled and tears gently ran down my cheeks.

Vaguely I was aware of the excited chatter of my companions, but I could not join in and I sat quietly embracing this heart-warming experience, this awareness of 'returning home', a moment that reinforced my belief in reincarnation.

Within a few minutes hot milky tea was served to us with an assortment of sweet biscuits and dried fruits, all beautifully presented in porcelain bowls with a blue lotus flower design painted on the side.

The lady shamans waited on us; there is no sex discrimination within the community regarding the recognition of a shaman. This power is recognized by the elders usually when the initiate is quite young and whether male or female they are given instruction and tuition by the established shamans.

These women, who were being so hospitable, were all wives and mothers; they integrated their shamanic duties with their family obligations. For them there was no conflict; both tasks were of equal importance and promoted happiness and well-being both within their immediate family and the whole community.

The ladies now waiting on us jingled their way in and out. Later we would see them complete their outfits with the addition of eagle-feathered headdresses.

Once they saw we had satisfied ourselves with the afternoon tea they joined us inside the yurt and along with Rollanda, who had until that point remained outside, they sat on the benches opposite.

Few minutes later a shape filled the open doorway and a woman entered. Without any need for announcement we knew immediately that this was the famed Ai-Churek.

She had a presence that was tangible, an aura of one with authority.

She waved a hand of greeting in our direction and then sat down on one of the benches alongside her fellow shamans. Her head was unadorned and her jet-black hair hung in two long pigtails.

Over the ever-popular black trousers, she was wearing a bright blue embroidered tunic, very mandarin in design and style.

On her feet were knee-high boots. These were made of an animal skin with the hair still on the outside, probably reindeer and the style was of the traditional Siberian one with a long curled-up toe. It was the jacket topping her outfit that was breathtaking. This surely must have been an original that had somehow evaded the destructive path of the Communist regime.

It was a black shiny fur skin with an overlaid design made of a longer light brown fur, and later when she stood up and turned around I saw that on the back of the jacket the decoration was clearly that of a large snake.

Small fur tails, seemingly stitched at random, also hung from this garment and what appeared to be ringlets of multicolored rags trimmed the lower edge.

She sat there and in silence surveyed us all. Who knows what she was thinking?

But as her eyes fixed on mine I felt she knew all there was to know about me for her eyes bored deep into my soul.

It was an experience I will never forget. There was nothing kept hidden.

In a flash she had scanned my life, she surveyed my sins and she recognized my talents; nothing had escaped.

There was a feeling of exposure but not of violation for I knew in an instance some of her power came from the fact that she would hold this knowledge, use it only for good and with her it would remain a secret unshared, but it was information she could use to guide and help.

Rollanda conversed in Russian with her for a while and then repeated the gist of it to us.

"Shortly we will be going to the town hall to see a performance by the famous Tuvan throat singers.

It is very fortuitous that you are here on this day, for this concert is for one night only. I know you will love this; it will be a wonderful experience. Afterwards we will return to this spot and witness the shamans performing the ceremony in which thanks are given to the sun for the day's appearance and which then moves on into a ceremony to greet and welcome the moon and stars."

She concluded by saying: "Please remain seated for the moment as Ai-Churek has a gift for each of you."

Once again I was struck by the generosity of the small communities that I visit around the world. The less they have the more they give and they truly find great joy in this act of giving. It comes from their heart.

Moon Heart stood up, her round face with its pale complexion reflecting her name, the darkness of her hair accentuating this contrast and adding to the image.

She reached into her voluminous robes and produced some small carved items, and then she took the few steps across the floor. Moving in front of us, she paused before deciding which item she passed over, for every gift was different.

As she came to me she turned her head and said something over her shoulder to one of the other shamans who immediately rose from her seat and hurried out of the yurt. Then indicating to me that there was something on the way she passed me by and continued to present a single gift to each of the rest of the group.

The messenger returned after a few minutes and passed something to this lady who had remained standing; she looked at it, nodded and then took the few steps back in my direction and handed it to me.

I received it with cupped hands and as I looked it rendered me speechless. Sitting in my palms was a soapstone replica of the beautiful coiled bronze panther on display in the museum. An identical one to that which Llyn was wearing, the one I had secretly lusted after since I first laid eyes on it.

Chapter 5

Expressing our thanks for the hospitality and the gifts, we got to our feet and prepared to leave, with Rollanda like a mother hen chivvying us along. As our guide and co-coordinator she was assuming her high schoolteacher's role and was trying to make sure we would not be late in arriving for the theatre performance.

Reluctantly we moved out of the yurt. This setting was one we were not anxious to leave, for to be sitting among these shamans was a moment we wished to prolong. By now there was a total of seven shamans in the yurt, all attired in their ceremonial robes, garments that were saturated with the energies of hundreds of rituals and ceremonies, and a sense of the power that surrounded them sat in the air.

For each of us present it was a unique moment and one to savor.

With the knowledge that we would be returning directly here once the concert had finished Rollanda had her way and bending our heads low we stepped out through the doorway and back into the heat.

In my hand I clasped the stone image of the coiled panther. I felt unable to put it in my bag or pocket. I felt it needed to be in my hand for it held great importance.

Why was this?

How could I have been given THIS item?

How do you describe such a happening?

This was more than coincidence, more than even synchronicity.

Who knew what was in my head and thoughts? The mind boggles.

Did Ai-Churek pick up some image there? Even if she had why should she respond to it unless there was something meaningful in the connection?

The panther had been a recurring image in my life for several years now and this always, I felt, came with a deep spiritual connection.

Several years previously, while at an auction and planning to buy furniture, I had found myself instead putting up my hand at the wrong time and discovering I had purchased a painting of a large black panther, posed with his head turned outwards and large golden eyes that seemed to look right into mine.

Just the previous year while attending a one-day shamanic workshop in London, this powerful animal unexpectedly joined me, albeit in spirit form and unwitnessed by the other participants; but to me it was as real and as solid as the person sitting next to me.

We left the area where the clinic was sited and continued to walk further on alongside the river, before turning inwards and heading for the theatre. All the while my companions' chatter sailed over my head and I found it impossible to contribute anything to the conversation.

The sense that I was on the brink of something special prevailed. It was impossible to say what, but a feeling of anticipation mixed with a large dose of trepidation sat in my stomach.

After a ten-minute walk we arrived at the theatre, which was a large stone building right in the center of the town. We entered and found it was totally packed, a full house with every seat taken and many of the smaller children sitting on their parents' laps, and the noise of the chatter filled the auditorium.

We must have been the last to arrive, but here we were treated like royalty and shown to reserved seats in the front row.

There was a buzz and an air of excitement filled the building. We sat down.

Moments later the large curtains swung open and on strode a small man robed in magnificent traditional Tuvan costume. He was accompanied by a great roar from the audience, which increased even more as he assumed a position center stage and threw both arms up in the air as a greeting.

He dazzled in his crimson satin robe, trimmed with silver embroidery that sparkled and shone, and around his waist was a bright orange cummerbund. He was wearing a hat in the same vivid color and shaped like a cross between a crown and a bishop's mitre. It was one that gave him a little height but this was physical height that he didn't need, for he had a huge presence. Stylish black boots with the long curled-up toes and more silver decoration completed his apparel.

His face had a full beam smile and as he reached center stage he threw his arms up wide and this symbolic gesture embraced us all and brought forth another great roar of welcome from everyone.

His huge personality had such an impact which in these few short moments belied his small stature.

This was the famous Kongar-ol Ondar newly returned from a highly successful tour of the USA. This exponent of the famous Tuvan throat singing had progressed far since winning the UNESCO throat singing championship in 1992, and a school he had founded was flourishing. He was also, we learned, a deputy in the Tuvan Parliament.

Throat singing in Tuva is a unique tradition and is where a soloist sings two, three or even four notes at once. There is a main note with the second an octave above and the sounds emitted can vary from a whistle to a growl. To hear this music performed by the most talented exponent of the art is an unforgettable experience.

This trip was already providing the most amazing abundance of gifts and dropping them right into our laps.

The joy and verve of this man who stood before us was infectious and he produced a program full of his most gifted and talented pupils. Not only did we relish the music, but also everyone who sat there in this vast auditorium was caught up in this man's infectious enthusiasm.

The show with children from the age of five dressed in full traditional costume and displaying their throat singing abilities was spectacular.

It knocked our socks off!!

Finally, it came to an end and everyone reluctantly departed from the building. As we walked outside, a TV crew was waiting and they asked Llyn if she would be willing to voice an opinion on the show and the music. She spoke on behalf of us all when she said, "It was absolutely amazing! We all loved it," and our nodding heads and broad smiles confirmed the pleasure the event had delivered.

The day was still not over and we made our way expectantly back to the Tungar Clinic.

Once again we entered the comforting appeal of the yurt where there is something womblike and soft about being inside a round dwelling and we settled ourselves on the cushions still in awe and full of praise for the singing event we had just witnessed.

Once we were settled the shamans, this time, served us a full meal. We were touched by their hospitality for we had come seeking to be their pupils, anxious to learn from them and they were treating us as honored guests.

Offerings of a platter full of mutton, dishes of potatoes prepared in various ways to make each look and taste different, big chunks of bread and a grand assortment of dried fruits were put in front of us. In a country where the ground is frozen solid for most of the year these generous people had prepared us a meal that offered us a sample of the best that this unforgiving land yields.

When we had finished eating, the bowls were cleared. Two of the women returned, one of them carrying a tray with small handle-less cups on it, and the other weighed down with the weight of a huge black iron kettle that somehow she managed to tip and pour for each of us, a drink of hot tea to aid the digestion.

Now it was time for the closing ceremony of the day and we got to our feet and filed out of the yurt.

These people still live close to Nature, like so many ancient cultures and for hundreds of years they have maintained a relationship with the sun and the moon and with the elements. Their healing powers are acquired through a constant communication and bonding with the spirits of Nature and the ancestors.

Daily they make a point of greeting the sun as it rises, and in the evening when it sets they will without fail offer a sign of appreciation for this life-giving source. Now we prepared to join them for the first time in this ritual.

But first they requested that the seven of us stand in a line, and we willingly complied, standing shoulder to shoulder. A small crowd of the local people had collected to observe the evening ceremony and stood silently staring at us as we stood expectantly.

Once more we were overwhelmed by the generosity of our Tuvan hosts, for they presented each of us with small porcelain drinking bowl, beautifully decorated with hand-painted lotus flowers and also around our necks they draped a Khata scarf.

The giving of this usually white silk scarf, with Buddhist symbols traced on it, is one I recognized from my stay in Ladakh. This traditional offering is constantly exchanged to enforce the greeting between two people in the East and symbolizes the wish for health and happiness. Our hosts were conveying this wish for us with the bestowing of this gift, but had added to it as these scarves were a glorious sun bright gold color.

With our scarves hanging from our necks and the bowls held carefully in our hands we were led to a couple of wooden benches that had been provided for us to sit on. Here at close quarters we could witness the closing ritual of the day.

In front of us a ring of stones surrounded a stack of wood and Rollanda began to describe the ceremony that was about to commence.

She started by informing us of the importance of the number nine in Tuvan shamanism and told us that even in laying wood for the fire this number is borne in mind. Each layer as the fire is prepared is made up of nine sticks and a male shaman always puts the first light to the fire. So often the reasons for such rituals are lost in the sands of time, but these are never questioned and the people accept that there lies a hidden importance which will forever remain.

The shamans were now all wearing an assortment of wonderful feathered headdresses to complement their robes, and they commenced to make a circle around the still unlit fire. They were all holding drums of varying sizes, some of which had designs painted on either the wood frame or the skin.

The crowd of local people gathered to watch the proceedings had grown, but the view of the setting sun would not be restricted for we were sitting with our backs to the Tungar Clinic building and beyond the fire only about 30 yards away, with the banks here free from trees, lay the broad river.

On the edge of this seemingly uninhabited tundra, which lay on the opposite side of this stretch of water, we could see the sun as it now rapidly dropped towards the horizon.

The one male shaman, whose name was Heurell, came forward and knelt in front of the woodpile. He struck a match and placed it underneath, then stood back, picked up his drum and gently sounded the first beat as he watched the flames begin to rise.

The women shamans then echoed the beat, slowly and softly at first and at this same pace they started to move around the fire; but as the flames began to rise into the air, both sound and tempo increased as their beaters hit the skins and matched the height of the flames.

Stamping their feet as they moved around the fire, spinning in circles, the drums and the clang from the metal rods hanging from their robes began to merge... the sun had now touched the horizon. The shamans began to chant and as they did so a great shudder went through me and I started to shake.

Before a shaman 'journeys' to other worlds they need to attain an altered state of consciousness and recent research has shown that if a drum is synchronized with brainwave frequencies it is easier to achieve this altered state, hence the importance of rhythmic drumming and chant in tribal cultures.

The drumming now, without any conscious effort on my part, was transporting me into this other level and the physical shaking rippled through me. I was totally caught up with the sound and the visual spinning of the shamans; like a child on a roundabout I was mesmerized.

Fortunately it went no further and I remained seated; gradually the drumming slowed and I felt able to open my eyes. The sun had disappeared below the horizon and the daylight was quickly fading. I watched as one by one the shamans stopped playing and placed their drums on the ground, where they then knelt beside them placing their foreheads on the ground. Finally, there was just a lone sound of the beat coming from the drum of Moon Heart, until with one final beat she too got to her knees and joined the others in this supplicant pose.

The crowd around us remained standing in silence until after a few minutes the shamans all got to their feet. Rollanda indicated for us to remain where we were, for the ceremony had not yet finished and we were instantly aware of the reason. A ritual commenced that we were to participate in for the first time and this was a beating.

We watched as Heurell and one of the other shamans each picked up a leather thronged flail and our eyes followed them as they began to use these instruments with well aimed practice across the backs of the spectators.

None of us escaped a whack on the back. This, although not painful, definitely stung and achieved its purpose of bringing us all back into an awareness of the physical and normal consciousness.

My spirit was well and truly back in my body.

I returned to the now, to the present moment as the encroaching darkness brought our first full day in Tuva to a close. What a day!

It was time for bed and without more ado we thanked our hosts and made haste for the hotel and our rooms.

As I awoke the following morning I instantly recalled a dream from the night. It was fresh in my mind and I saw it all clearly.

I had seen an expanse of land with a mass of the most exquisite tiny bright blue flowers and I could also see each one as if it were held right in front of my eyes, for they had just four petals in the shape of a cross. The detail was very vivid and I tucked the image away in my memory library.

We gathered at breakfast and all of us after a good night's sleep were this morning refreshed and raring to go and to let the adventure continue. Today we would be heading out into the Steppes and for the next few days we would be traveling with the shamans and living in yurts.

We had a long way to go but first, before we set off, we wanted to acquire some drums.

Gisela and Llyn had brought their own with them, Mike and Jennifer were borrowing spare ones from the shamans and Sam, Diane and I were hoping to purchase ours in the town.

We cleared our rooms and loaded our bags onto the coach, and set off with Rollanda directing the driver to the shop where we hoped to make our purchases.

We found it without any problem. It was very small, but we were thankful that at least it was open, for there seemed to be no set opening hours for anything in this small town. Inside, on shelves and in the glass-topped counter cabinets were an assortment of trinkets, carvings and embroidered bags. Our interpreter asked if they had any drums and with a moment of serendipity the shopkeeper produced three, the total amount he had for sale and he set them out in a row. As I looked at them I saw that the smallest one had a snake painted along the wooden rim, and as I picked it up and turned it over I saw that this image was also carved onto the crossbar.

The snake has played an important role in my spiritual development and this symbol holds great personal meaning. There was no question in my mind that this drum had been sitting there waiting for me.

I held onto it and immediately said to Sam and Diane, "This is the one I would like," and they raised no objection.

The other two drums were both the same size and appeared to have no difference, and then Sam put her hand on one and said, "I feel drawn to this one." Diane shrugged her shoulders, happy to accept the remaining one.

We each pulled out our wallets and passed over the requested amount of money. And as Sam lifted her drum from the counter she turned it over and to our surprise on the crossbar of it was a burnt-in emblem… It was that of an arrow… the spiritual tool that I had retrieved for her just a couple of days earlier.

She laughed; who would question that this drum belonged to her? Such confirmation never loses its magic.

The third drum, that Diane now owned, had no paintings and no decoration. It was totally blank and somehow this seemed to reflect the stage of her life that she was now at, for she had just resigned from her job and within a few days of her return to the USA, she would be embarking on a new career, and she was also moving house. It was an empty canvas for her to start anew.

The three of us were thrilled with our drums, but as we turned to leave the shop there was another surprise for me. As I gave a last glance around there was something that caught my eye, and in one of the side glass-topped counters I spotted a carved wooden mask, just one and it was an effigy of the Maha Kala!

This deity that had appeared to me and had also at one time morphed his energy into my physical body. This Tibetan force that I knew so little about but one that was constantly intruding into my days... I simply had to buy it.

This image showed him with a bright red face with his three bulbous eyes, one of which is in the center of his forehead. His mouth was open and the fanged teeth, two on the bottom and two on the top, were ready to devour anything he chose. Across the top of his head was a crown of five white-painted, red-eyed skulls, and from each of his extended earlobes hung a gold eight-petaled lotus flower.

With a drum in one hand and the mask of the deity sometimes called the White Protector clutched to my bosom, I climbed back onto the coach.

If my companions were puzzled at my purchase they made no comment.

I knew this painted wooden image, however fearful it appeared, would be a daily nudge to constantly remind me of the magical unseen world that surrounds us and the vastness of our Universe.

I felt drawn to keep this mask on view, rather than put it in my bag, and with great reverence I placed it on the top of the coach dashboard facing outwards as if clearing the way and disposing of anything untoward in our path.

From the shop we drove directly to the Tungar Clinic where we joined forces with the shamans. They were waiting outside surrounded by assorted boxes and buckets containing food and water, sleeping bags and tents and all the necessities for the forth-coming trip. Then with several of the shamans including Ai-Churek joining us on the coach, we set off. Our convoy resembled a traveling circus, for there was our coach, plus two other vans, and along with the occupants were drums, flails, several large feathered headdresses and an assortment of shamanic regalia.

We were headed out into the Steppe, beginning an adventure

into who knew what, just going where the path led, holding onto the belief that we were in the right place at the right time and that our destiny was being fulfilled.

Within minutes we were out of the town and out of sight of any habitation. In this climate people mostly prefer not to live in total isolation. The tundra rolled away in all directions, with just the sight of a few sparsely wooded areas and mountains always in the distance. The road lying like a ribbon in front of us was the only visible clue that man had passed this way before.

Accompanying Moon Heart on our coach was her apprentice, a young Russian girl with blond hair and the very palest blue eyes. Her name was Natasha and the intent was that she would live constantly and closely with this powerful shaman for two years, away from her family and any social distraction. This young girl's time would be spent watching and learning all aspects of shamanism from her teacher. Already after one year she was beginning to be recognized in her own right as a healer with exceptional talent.

Two of the other women shamans, Nadia and Vera, had also found seats on our bus and now out of their ceremonial robes they had assumed their secondary roles and were for the moment just two friends enjoying the opportunity to abandon the household chores and go on an excursion into the country.

Vera, we would discover, had a beautiful singing voice and in the next few days would delight us with a range of songs.

I gazed out of the window at the seemingly deserted landscape and in the skies, defying this notion, I saw several eagles soaring and drifting as their sharp eyes scanned the land below for the next meal.

The bus bumped and rocked along the rough road and after we had been traveling for about an hour Moon Heart, carefully holding onto the backs of the seats, made her way to the front where I was seated. With a few words in Russian she passed me an object wrapped in a chiffon scarf; then turning swayed her way back to her seat. She paused halfway and pointed out of the coach to something on the left-hand side, again speaking in Russian.

Rollanda, who was sitting across the aisle opposite me, offered us the translation.

"Some five miles in that direction is a sacred place that is highly beneficial to women with infertility-related problems. The land there is wet and boggy and part of the healing treatments consists of totally immersing the patient in the mud!"

What other rituals were also included into the overall treatment she didn't say, nor did she reveal exactly how long the patient has to remain covered in mud.

However, she did add, "The high success rate is undisputed and many women arriving with infertility problems have become pregnant shortly after undergoing treatment here."

I puzzled over this information. A sacred and powerful spot. But it was so far from habitation. Who discovered it? How did they learn of its powers?

Questions such as these I have learned do not bother shamans; they simply accept the miracles that our planet reveals.

Our interpreter then turned her attention to me. I had unwound the material which remained attached and tied at one end to the article I had been given and in my hand now lay a carved spoon. It was made from a light colored wood, about 12 inches long and had a patina shine that only comes from frequent use. The bowl of this piece of carving was square and flat with nine small indentations, and the handle had intricate carving of a geometric design.

She looked at the item in my hand and I heard her say, "Aaaah. That is an offering spoon, used when we salute the spirits of the earth.

Moon Heart has taken that one many times to Italy and used it in countless ceremonies."

I was thrilled to have been given such a precious gift, but the logical question was... why? And why me?

An inexplicable feeling arose, an unquantifiable sense that in a far distant past my life and that of this shaman had been closely connected. As I smoothed out the gray-white and black mottled material before rewrapping the spoon, I saw that it was in fact a snakeskin print... These continuous links and connections I felt were non-random events, but had a special meaning; however, at the moment this meaning was still unclear.

I rested my head back against the seat and gazed out of the window at the passing landscape. There was a lot of chatter going on but I felt disinclined to join in and allowed my thoughts to freely float in and out of my head.

We traveled on through this vast tract of land entertained by Vera's beautiful singing. And with only a few enforced stops for minor vehicle maintenance, which proved a welcome relief as it provided the opportunity to escape from the carbon monoxide fumes that I knew were invading the inside of the vehicle, to stretch our legs and breathe in some clean fresh air.

By the afternoon we reached the mountains that had been but a speck in the distance when we commenced our journey, and had already been climbing upwards for quite a while when we arrived at a narrow pass.

Here from this high vantage point we could look back on the road we had traveled, and by turning also see the way ahead as it continued down into a new valley.

A point such as this is highly venerated by the Tuvan people and it was indeed quite magical.

To our surprise a small group of people were waiting to greet us with a picnic lunch. Rollanda told us they had come from a nearby village, but the word 'nearby' in these remote areas has for them a totally different understanding and usage than ours, living as we do in our suburban homes.

However, there is no lack of communication in these sparsely populated areas. Even before the advent of cell phones news travels fast, and although there is often a great time discrepancy between the moment set for a planned event and its commencement, this is met with a resigned acceptance.

Here it is all in the lap of the gods.

On the side of a mountain, in this magnificent setting, we were again provided with a feast. Once we the travelers were filled and rested, and before we moved further, it was time to offer thanks to the spirits of the place, to keep them appeased and ask for their continued guidance and protection as we traversed another region of this vast country.

A large fir tree standing solitary on this pass was testament to the importance attached to this site as from previous thanksgivings it was already bedecked with votive rags and ribbons and with its finery resembled a child in a party dress.

In front of the tree was a circle of stones and the ground held signs that many fires had been lit within its confines.

We all shared in the task of gathering any scrap of dry dead wood to add to the small bundle the shamans had brought with them to provide another fire, placing it in front of Heurell who assumed the responsibility of laying the sticks in the appropriate format.

Rollanda then told us, "Moon Heart has asked me to tell you that she would be happy for you all to participate in the ceremony so have your bowls and drums ready."

With great anticipation we watched as the shamans then pulled out bags and boxes from the vans and transformed themselves as they donned their shamanic robes and feathered headdresses.

We Westerners were dressed comfortably but conservatively in slacks and shirts, however we got out the golden Khata scarves we had been gifted, and either tied them around our waists or had them draped around our necks to add a little color to our apparel and we stood expectantly waiting for instruction.

I noticed that these shamans each had a wooden offering

spoon, similar to my gift, hanging from their belts, and when I had clambered back into the coach to get my scarf and bowl I had retrieved mine, and now this in similar fashion was tied by the snake-print scarf to the belt tab on my trousers.

My eyes never left the scene unfolding before me, for growing up without siblings, my childhood had been somewhat solitary and I discovered early on that much of learning is by observation.

Rollanda waved us forward. "It is time to begin," she said.

First we were given three lengths of plaited rag and following her verbal instruction commenced by tying each of these onto the sacred fir tree, and as we did so we silently requested the spirits to guard and bless us on our continuing journey. Next we lined up and holding out our bowls waited as Natasha poured a little milk into each of them.

"The milk is to be flicked into each of the four directions," continued Rollanda. "Watch how the shamans do it. This is an offering to the spirits of the mountains."

This was the use for the spoons the shamans all carried and for the one now in my care. We all entered respectfully into the spirit of the ritual. I was using my gift for the first time while my companions were flicking the milk with their fingers as we had done previously.

Once this ritual was completed to Moon Heart's satisfaction then the remainder of the milk was offered to the earth and poured on the ground, the spoons were left to hang from our belts and the shamans picked up their drums.

Rollanda was precise in her instructions to us, "Wait until all the shamans are beating and then join in following the momentum."

In this powerful setting we were drawn into the occasion and there was the feeling that the elements were recognizing this event for as we drummed there was a simultaneous, far off rumbling of thunder and a strong wind blew up that had been missing all the while we had been sitting in this spot enjoying our picnic.

At this point in our travels we were unaware that the land was in dire need of rain, that there had been small outbreaks of forest fires and that the shamans we were traveling with were incorporating a request for rain into their ceremonies.

There had been no significant rainfall in this area for over three months and the continuing dry spell was making the risk of fire become a major fear. Any fire started now could spread rapidly and unchecked for untold miles.

Meanwhile, with our fire safely contained within a ring of stones it continued to burn before it slowly diminished as we circled around it without a break in the drumming for maybe thirty minutes. Then I was aware that the tempo was slowing and one by one the shamans stopped moving, turned to face the fire and stood still. Then as they had done the evening before they laid down their drums, and getting onto their knees placed their foreheads on the ground and we all followed suit.

A solitary beat from Moon Heart continued for a few moments before she too laid down her drum and knelt beside it.

This was the end of the ceremony, except for the flail. The use of this was the responsibility of Heurell and today seemed a fitting conclusion as he ensured no lingering unsought energies remained attached to any of us.

The shamans quickly removed their sacred robes, repacked the vans and checked and double-checked the site of the fire before satisfying themselves no lingering embers remained before we set off again.

Another two hours into our drive and we stopped once more for another small ritual. I had purposely left my wristwatch in my case and had by now lost all sense of time. In this part of the world in June there is daylight for twenty of the twenty-four hours and I was now on shamanic time.

As we climbed down from the bus, which had pulled off the

road, I saw we were in the middle of a great plain, an expanse of golden-green grass and parked by the side of a small copse of trees. These at first glance seemed to be a combination of just silver birch and fir.

At the front of this group of trees standing alone and about fifty feet from the others was a small single tree, some specimen of fir but unlike those others growing close by. For whatever reason this one had obviously been declared special for it was wearing the now familiar robe of ribbons and in front of it was a small pile of stones, stones that I guessed would over time grow into a fair sized ovaa. Into crevices or simply placed on these stones and rocks were the offerings and these were in the form of cigarettes and also of coins.

Smoke is used in shamanic rituals and sacred ceremonies all over the world, either from a small wood fire, cigarette or pipe, or from an incense burner. Again no one questions it; it is an ancient ritual that has always been with us.

I understand that smoke is used as a cleansing element, but I feel there is some further lost wisdom in the necessity for it. On many occasions I have witnessed healers who although they never smoke socially will incorporate cigarette or pipe smoking into a healing session and candles are an integral part of every celebration worldwide and may be the remnants of a lost ritual.

We followed the shamans as they walked across the grass and into the small copse, into a clearing, and as directed we sat down.

For a while we simply sat there in silence, breathing in the fresh air and watching the branches of the trees gently sway.

After the noise of the bus engine and the chatter of a lot of women it was very relaxing. There was no ceremony but these people living so close to nature understand the importance of finding these moments of solitude when we can obliterate the constant distractions and listen to the little voice inside of us, the voice of our own innate wisdom.

We waited for Moon Heart to make the first move and then

with some reluctance we all started to get to our feet. As I turned to put my hand on the soil to help myself back onto my feet I spotted a patch of blue. Looking closer I saw nestling in the grass a cluster of growing plants sprouting and topped by a beautiful cross-shaped flower. It was the flower that had been shown to me in last night's dream, a flower that I was to discover could be found in only two places in the world. It grows out here on the Siberian Steppe and can also be found at the base of some mountains in Switzerland.

This land was speaking to me, through my dreams and through my eyes.

Then on we traveled, arriving at a large village just over an hour later. Our caravan of vehicles turned into a field that had been designated as the village sports stadium. At either end were white-painted goal posts and halfway down on one side was a three-tiered wooden structure, a stand, not worthy of the adjective 'grand' for it was no more than 12 feet long, with four stepped planks, but it served its purpose for on this were seated a handful of people.

In the middle of the field stood a yurt. It looked slightly out of place but we were happy to get off the bus and away from the heat and fumes that had increased uncomfortably during the day.

We visitors along with Galena were invited into the yurt and happy to sit in its carpeted interior; the discomfort of the bus and the long hours traveling had been very tiring.

Again the hospitality of the Tuvan people was overwhelming: we were immediately brought in hot drinks and then the food started arriving. While we were being feted I noticed that Rollanda, along with Moon Heart and the other shamans, was standing outside a short distance away and although I could neither hear nor understand the language I could see from the body language that they were having a heated conversation.

After a while they walked away in the direction of a small group of wooden houses that lay just beyond the perimeter of the field.

About half an hour later we were sated and sat waiting for Rollanda to return. Although still light it was very late in the day and we wanted to know where we would be staying overnight.

Was it here?

Or did we still have further to go?

Had the purchase of our drums been only this morning?

That seemed impossible!

It had been an extremely long day and the combination of the heat and traveling, the ceremonies, with jet lag thrown in, was all beginning to tell; we were all struggling to keep awake, let alone make conversation.

It was at this point that Rollanda reappeared; she sat down in front of us looking somewhat embarrassed. She started talking and with a diplomatic and persuasive manner she set out a proposed plan. We were somewhat taken aback for this is what she said:

"Moon Heart has asked that you as Western shamans do some healing on a few of the villagers. They are very interested to see how you work and wish to see how powerful you are. They have been waiting a long time for you to come and they feel it is a great honor for the village.

Please understand that those who have requested a healing from you are really very brave, for they have no idea what you will do to them and most of them have never seen anyone from the West.

These humble villagers have great faith in the words of Moon Heart and she has told them you are good shamans. If we want to exchange ideas and values and gain a greater understanding of each other's cultures this is where it must begin. A compatibility between our governments can only be achieved when the people demand it.

Everything has to start at grass roots level."

Of course everything she said was true, but the request had

been thrust upon us and was totally unexpected.

We were stunned; we had come here to learn, expecting to watch and be instructed. There were mutterings, but Llyn immediately took charge.

"Rollanda, I really don't think we can, we are all desperately tired. There was never any suggestion that we would perform healings. As individuals we work differently, we each have sacred items that are special to us that we use in our work and all of these artifacts have been left safely at home."

Our interpreter stood facing Llyn. "This community has been waiting for the shamans from the West to arrive for many days. Moon Heart has already told them you will do some healings." Her attitude was confrontational.

Poor Llyn, in that moment her quality as a leader showed itself. We were still on our first day of traveling with Ai-Churek who was reputed to possess a temperamental and difficult personality. But the opportunity to watch this unique shaman in action was within our grasp and to upset her now presented the possibility of her refusing to go any further with us.

Llyn took a deep breath and looked around at us. "Perhaps we could do just the one?"

Before we could answer we heard Rollanda say, "There are already four people waiting!"

With the wisdom of Solomon, Llyn countered with, "How about if we work together as a group and do a group healing?"

We were all less than enthusiastic but to refuse further would have been churlish. There was a need to support Llyn and so we weakly agreed.

It was then that Gisela said, "I prefer to work alone, so I will take one patient."

With a sigh of relief Llyn moved in with, "Okay. Mike, Jennifer and I have worked together recently with the Tamayos, we will use their methods."

Then thinking as she spoke she looked at Sam and said,

"Would you, Diane and Wendy drum to raise the energy and assist us in that way?"

A tricky situation had been averted and making a supreme effort we focused on the task ahead.

Chapter 6

Gisela set off by herself to collect and prepare whatever she needed for the individual healing, while the rest of us worked together as a group. As we talked, we each contributed ideas and suggestions and soon a plan was formulated.

I was happy to assist with a drummer's role. I had been fortunate enough to have twice visited and been witness to the powerful work of the Tamayo shamans who live in the shadow of active volcanoes and was keen to observe how Llyn, Mike and Jennifer would adapt their methods.

Here we were unable to call on the energies of those snowcapped mountains, but we had spent the day traveling over the great mountains of Tuva and through dark fir forests. Here we had also marveled at the vastness of the sky when we traversed the plain, so now we called on the spirits of this land, the land that surrounded us.

First Llyn asked Rollanda to see if she could acquire some eggs. Many South American shamans use eggs that they roll over the patient's body to draw off the negative energies and these together with smudging, which is smoke from burning sage that is blown over the patient, would be used as the cleansing agents.

Then she turned to us and said, "Let's first decide where we will work." We moved out of the yurt, looked around and as we walked we found an area that we all agreed felt comfortable. It was part of the field that to the eye looked no different from the rest, but when you are working with unseen energies, the instinctive sense of feeling is one that comes into play and needs to be listened to.

"Right," she continued. "Let's find some large stones and mark out a circle. Make a boundary that we will work within."

Once this was accomplished we walked to the perimeter of the field where a few small bushes were growing and from these we picked a bundle of thin stemmed, leaf filled branches.

The branches we fashioned into natural flails. In my lengthy travels I am constantly reminded how a core element is embodied in the rituals performed by shamans worldwide. The 'beating' is the closing part of healing rituals performed by shamans living high in the Andes. Yesterday and again today I had witnessed it being the final part of a ritual enacted in the middle of Siberia.

As we made our way back to the spot we had chosen as a working place I noticed a large feather lying on the ground which I picked up. It's a habit I seem to have always had for the altar set up in my home is adorned with feathers, white baby ones that proliferate in spring, sleek glossy black ones from the crow family and several beautiful 'eyes' discarded from a male peacock.

The new one now in my hand had its own unique beauty with hairs in shades of brown and cream and had once soared in the skies attached to an eagle; now I stuck it in my belt.

We sat down in the now-prepared healing circle as Llyn talked through the form the healing ritual would take: the cleansing, the extraction, the healing and the blessing. Then after a short meditation we walked to the coach and collected our drums.

As I started to step down from the coach I spotted the newly purchased wood carving of the Maha Kala where he had spent the day in the front window and also picked him up. Then as we walked back to our stone circle there was a noticeable increase in the number of people gathering in the field. Many more had arrived, word had spread and it seemed almost all of the villagers had turned out to look at this strange group of people who had come from a land halfway round the world.

I propped up the image of the Tibetan deity against the largest stone and instantly a sense of his presence seemed to dominate the circle.

We were ready to start, Rollanda and Galena were on hand to interpret and Llyn requested that the spectators keep well to the outside of the ring of stones to allow us space.

Llyn had specified that a maximum of four of the local people who had requested a healing could be treated and these were now identified. Gisela stepped forward, took one of the ladies by the hand and led her away in the search of somewhere private. She requested no observers, and as a proficient speaker of Russian envisaged no problems.

The other three volunteer patients consisted of two ladies and one man, and they were invited to step forward into the middle of the circle and stand in a line. Mike, Jennifer and Llyn then moved and each stood opposite one while both of the interpreters remained close by.

With a nod from Llyn we began to gently drum and Sam, Diane and I walked slowly around the perimeter of the circle giving our healers the maximum amount of room and keeping close to the edge of the standing spectators.

As the healers began their work the energy remained at one level for a while then there was an almost imperceptible shift. We were sited at the edge of the field and I became aware of a light wind suddenly arrive, and as I looked up I saw it rustling through the leaves on the overhanging tree branches.

Suddenly I felt this unseen force increase and in a few short minutes it became quite strong. The strength of it grew rapidly; it seemed to enfold me and as it did so my breathing changed and I began to take continuous huge breaths and as I did I felt my chest expanding. It was as if I was physically growing not particularly in height, but in girth!

Accompanying this came the real sensation of my torso thickening and strengthening. It was not only the upper part of my body that was affected for suddenly my legs felt short and squat. In an instant, there was an overwhelming realization that the powerful energy of what I later came to recognize was the physical embodiment of the Maha Kala was moving into my body and using me as a means to empower the ceremony.

Instantly, having found a vehicle to use, it took but a moment to fully arrive.

This is the most difficult sensation to describe and our English language is devoid of the words to do it justice. It was not an 'out of body' experience, because I am not on the outside viewing myself. But at the same time there is a definite detachment; I know what my body is doing but the power that moves into it overrules all of my control. There is no element of self-consciousness because the 'everyday me' plays no part in the proceedings. It is as if I have willingly surrendered my body. I seem to step back and be secondary to the wishes of some higher power. Often when I review these similar but infrequent incidents I wonder if an arrangement was agreed upon before I took on human form and started the journey that is this lifetime.

When I 'lose' my body to these higher powers it happens without warning, without planning, without a request from either side, it is instantaneous and once the task is complete it departs in a likewise manner.

As the wind had started to increase, I suddenly stopped playing and had turned and carefully placed my drum on the ground, leaning it against a tree. Later I remembered physically performing this act, but it was guided by a source outside of me, from far beyond my normal conscious level, for I had no reason to do so. My body then instantly went into some sort of ritualistic dance. I was vaguely aware of what was happening but not in control of any of my actions.

The feedback from witnesses once these happenings are over is always interesting and the description relating to this occasion is theirs.

"She stomped and circled, with knees bent and her feet splayed out. Her hands reached above her head as if she was retrieving something, then the fingers would close and with clenched fists she seemed to pull whatever it was down from the Heavens. This energetic display was accompanied by loud calls and deep-throated grunting."

When the energy, of its own volition, withdrew from me I experienced a feeling like a balloon deflating, a definite departing of something unseen and I felt myself move back into control of my thoughts and actions.

Slowly I walked out of the circle, through the crowd which parted to let me pass and I moved a few feet away and then sat down on the grass. It was only for a brief time, as I needed only minutes to rest before I got back to my feet, retrieved my drum and resumed my role as a supporter.

It was shortly after this that Llyn brought the healing session to a close and the patients, after bowing deeply, turned to walk away. The crowd parted and as they passed between their neighbors and friends they were nodding and smiling. There was a positive air about them and the crowd of observers standing around us also broke up and began to form smaller groups before they wandered off across the field.

We stood for a while talking. Llyn seemed very happy at the way the ceremony had panned out. We had fulfilled our obligation and somehow we had our own reward, for the energy that had been generated had reinvigorated us all and the desperate tiredness that we had been experiencing earlier seemed to have totally vanished.

First we put our drums and the carving of the Maha Kala safely back in the bus, which remained parked on the outside of the field, before we strolled back in to where the activity was now centered.

We had all got our second wind and instead of being more tired than we were before we worked, we were keen to now witness what was going on and we chatted as we walked towards the wooden stand of seats partway along the field where the focus of events now was.

All of the Tuvan shamans were collected there; they had changed once more from their traveling clothes and had again donned their full shamanic robes and headdresses.

As we drew nearer we saw that they had several small sacks and were passing out handfuls of what looked like grain and dried fruit to the community, all of whom from the aged to the very young had formed a long line and were patiently waiting their turn. Once they had received this token gift they moved across and joined their companions, who were now patiently standing behind a single rope barrier that was pegged out to form a large circle.

In the center of this circle was another small stone circle and within this a stack of wood was laid ready for a fire to be lit and resting against these stones were the shamans' drums and beaters. Here was the indication that further events were planned; there was still more to come.

Some of the villagers were seated on the rickety 'grandstand' and they shuffled up making space for us to join them. We accepted their invitation and sat down and waited.

Finally the line of patient people waiting for the small food gift was extinguished and the community was now standing three to four deep outside of the rope ring.

The shamans twisted the necks of the now almost empty sacks and tied them tightly with string, put them close together and rested the small metal scoops on top of them. They then turned their attention to the next event and walked in towards the roped circle.

My eyes were drawn to Moon Heart, who had waited until last and I watched her don her magnificent headdress. This act seemed to empower her and irrespective of the added height it gave her, she grew in stature. Like a parting of the waters, a gap appeared in the spectators and she strode into the center of the circle. An expectant hush descended as she slowly turned around and looked at everyone.

Then she started to speak.

Like a legendary orator her voice boomed out. Rollanda translated very quickly for us and we were only fractionally behind the locals in what we were hearing.

She continued as if giving an empowered sermon from a High Church pulpit. This respected shaman spoke of the importance of having the right morals and care within the community, but in no way did she dictate. Her love and understanding of these people shone through with every word and they in turn listened intently.

She shared with them her understanding of the continuous struggle to survive in this harsh climate, aware of the importance of a good harvest and the growing desperation as the drought of this year continued. All of the shamans, she told them, were making many rituals to the Rain Spirits and to the ancestors requesting them to change this situation.

Then I heard Rollanda give us the shaman's final words. These were words which made my mouth drop open, for Moon Heart had given these people a promise. This was a promise which really put her reputation on the line for the translation was, "I am in communication with these unseen spirits, the spirits who occupy other realms and in three days' time there will be rain."

I looked up into what was still a clear and cloudless sky, but such was the power of her oratory it left me in no doubt of her conviction.

We sat waiting; this speech had now concluded but the crowd remained and it was obvious the shamans would now perform a ceremony. However, Rollanda's words had us back on our feet as we heard her say, "You have been invited to take part and join the shamans in their dance. Where are your drums?"

These words evoked a lot of excitement in us all and we jumped up to go and quickly collect our drums from the bus. We were back in a few minutes and stood expectantly. Rollanda, following directions from Ai-Churek, then instructed us to enter the roped-off circle.

My friends all very keen, moved quickly, but for some reason I felt the need to stay where I was; it was as if my feet were rooted to the ground and I didn't move.

I remained standing in the midst of the community, trying to ignore the blatant stares of the children.

"Come on, Wendy," called Sam as she followed the rest of the group and they ducked under the rope and into the circle, but I shook my head.

It was as if an invisible barrier had arisen and I remained where I stood.

Although the crowd were several people deep I would have a clear view of the events for the Tuvans are very small in stature and even the adult men were below my 5'3".

My friends stood with the other shamans around the central stack of wood as Heurell bent down, set it alight and I watched the flames shoot up. The regular and rhythmic sound of the drumbeats followed and as the robed shamans started to move around the fire, I watched my friends follow their lead and become part of the ceremony. Soon the loud mesmerizing calls of these Siberian shamans filled the air, a great shudder went through me, and I felt the hairs on my head and arms stand on end.

It was powerful stuff.

Almost seconds later there was a sudden disruption. It happened suddenly and right beside me, as a young girl suddenly keeled over and passed out and the attention of the spectators around her was diverted from the main event.

Spread out at my feet lay this young person; she was on her back, arms by her side totally straight. She appeared to have fainted, but this was no normal buckling of the knees and a downward collapse; she had keeled over backwards as if struck on the forehead and fallen exactly as she had stood.

In an instant Nina, one of the shamans, had left the circle and was there. She was at the girl's side almost before she hit the ground and certainly before anyone realized what had happened and called her.

It was extraordinary.

From my viewpoint I saw the whole event and no one had called for help.

Nina, who one moment was immersed in her drumming and dancing, had almost bi-located so swift was her response and her actions staggered me.

I watched, as swiftly she moved behind the head of the prone figure, then bent over, reached down and grabbed the girl's long dark hair into both of her hands and by this means only pulled her a couple of feet along the ground. All the time she was shouting loudly and ferociously. Then she took a deep breath and repeated the process, and then finally with her hands still wrapped around the child's hair and using only this as a means, she literally lifted her onto her feet. All the while she continued emitting these almost deafening shouts.

Nina then looked at me and the fact that neither of us spoke the same language was immaterial, for I knew she was passing the care of this child over to me and together we moved through the crowd to the benches where I sat down on the bottom step with the young girl. Nina shot me a glance before she immediately returned to the drumming circle.

It had all happened so quickly. A few of the villagers close to where it had occurred had now turned around and were staring at the child, who was small, slightly built and looked to be about eleven years old. Others had refocused on the main event, and the majority of the people were totally unaware that anything untoward had occurred.

I could feel the child trembling slightly and I put my arm around her, but she was totally unresponsive; she sat ramrod straight unblinking and was staring straight ahead. Bending my head slightly forward I could see she was devoid of expression and her eyes were blank.

Suddenly Nina was back in front of us and, stepping between the child and the person on the other side of her, she stood on the bench behind and slightly above us. She bent forward and with both hands swept the long dark hair of the child up to the crown of the head, gathered it together and with great strength used this means to lift her bodily. This time the girl let out a yell; again Nina repeated the action and by this means lifted her up onto her feet whereupon a louder yell was emitted. This time the shaman seemed satisfied with her actions and the result she had produced, and without any comment or further pause she returned swiftly to the centerpiece ritual.

The child sat back down, but now looked around with a dazed expression, almost as if she had been suddenly awoken from a deep sleep. She put both hands to her head and spoke in Russian to one of her young companions who had been witness to this unusual display. I thought she was complaining of a headache, but in fact her prime concern was for the loss of her hairband. With this safely recovered from between the feet of some spectators, she happily slid it back into her hair and remained seated next to me regaining her interest in the proceedings.

I sat there also just watching; occasionally taking a sideways glance at the young girl whose name I learnt was Marina, which coincidentally is my second name. She seemed fine and there was no obvious sign that the dramatic events had disturbed her in any way. Now my focus was drawn to the fire and the circling of the shamans, the drumming and the chanting. It felt as if the drums were calling my name, I was being drawn in and suddenly there was an overwhelming desire to join in and integrate with that moving circle.

As has happened so many times my rational mind entered a see-saw conflict with a voice coming from a subconscious level. On one hand I was happy to remain where I was, but the pull to move was growing ever stronger.

It was like a magnet that I was unable to resist.

But leaving my drum where it was, I moved trance-like through a gap in the crowd and as I ducked under the rope to enter the circle I picked up a bead-filled rattle that was lying on the ground.

The moment I straightened up a huge force from an unknown source engulfed me. This was a totally different energy from the power that the Maha Kala had filled me with less than an hour previously. This was a sensuous, controlled power. I felt myself elongate, as if I was growing taller and my body started to sway and writhe and gyrate from the hips. Without any direct mental instruction and, as an observer of myself, I became aware that my arms, hands and fingers were weaving and waving.

I began to hiss.

Then snakelike I moved around the interior of the circle close to the spectators, facing them, and with my back to the continuing ceremony, but every so often I would pause, shake the rattle and my neck would seem to stretch and extend upwards. As this happened I would feel my body incline backwards, my chin would tuck in, then suddenly with a swift movement my head would move sharply and dramatically forward.

It was a cobra striking out!

I witnessed that those nearest would recoil with horror on their faces, but I felt absolutely emotionless and detached from all that was occurring.

In this manner I completed the total circle, right to where I had entered. Then still without any thought and a sense of total detachment I found myself turning in towards the center where I walked to the edge of the fire, got down on my knees and placed my forehead to the ground.

With this action and connection to the earth I felt the force within me become liquid-like and flow out of my body and return to Pachamama.

At this point I seemed to rejoin with my body and I became

conscious of where I was and aware that the tempo of the drums was slowing. As I slowly lifted my head the sound finally stopped and I saw that one by one the shamans were all walking towards the center and joining me, close to the fire's edge.

The shamans gently placed their tambours on the ground and then sank to their knees placing their foreheads on the ground, with my traveling companions following suit. Moon Heart remained standing, observing them all, and then she too moved to the fire and performed this reverent action.

The ceremony was complete and as one we all got back on our feet.

With its closure Nina immediately returned to check on the young girl. Moon Heart was close on her heels, swiftly removing the magnificent eagle feathered headdress and passing it into Natasha's care as she hurried to join her.

I turned and followed them and observed these two women as they sat down with Marina and with great gentleness they questioned her. Llyn and the rest of the group joined us by the small wooden terrace and Rollanda had also appeared. She stood close beside them, listening intently, but for the time being avoided any distraction to the procedure by not translating.

After about ten minutes, Rollanda led us away from the girl, the shamans and a large group of the villagers who were standing around still watching and silently listening.

Once we were a suitable distance away our guide gave us an explanation of what they felt had occurred.

This young girl had indeed fallen into what I had suspected and what is referred to as a shamanic trance. In communities here the role of shaman still holds great importance and this trance state is recognized as a good and powerful sign. It is a display that signifies a potential healer, the first indication that a child's future destiny is as a shaman. The spirits and ancestors are showing the community that this is a child who needs special tuition, care and guidance; the role that they have been chosen to play is a difficult one that will take them over a course that is hard and dangerous, but it is also a path that is impossible to refuse or reject.

They have no option for they have been called by the spirits.

Marina had been taken on her first journey to another realm; the shamans would discover whether she had visited the upper or the lower worlds, but either way, it was a hazardous excursion. Somehow, Nina, in the midst of her attention being totally focused on the rainmaking ceremony, had been invisibly directed to come to the aid of this child. She recognized what to the untrained eye would appear to have been a faint for what it truly was, and had reached into this other world of non-reality and literally pulled the conscious level of the child back into her body.

How different from the treatment one would receive in our society. A child or young adult suddenly going into a trance and then relating tales of other worlds would immediately be dispatched to a doctor, prescribed some form of medication and at worst hospitalized and kept sedated. The word unbalanced or psychotic would become a label that would probably stick for the rest of their life.

What a day! This had been a very long one and finally the light was beginning to fade which meant it was close to midnight and we still had further to travel.

Rollanda and all of the Tuvan shamans we were traveling with remained at the village and we assumed they would be spending the night there.

But Galena joined the rest of us as we wearily climbed back into our coach.

We were told we only had a few miles to go, but this information must have referred to the shorter distance as the crow flies. Unfortunately we were in a bus and at the mercy of the terrain, for soon we had left any semblance of a road behind.

Here in the middle of Tuva, in the darkness, we were looking for a nomadic family who were living in two yurts and we were following tracks that would have been testing for horses.

But such is the power of positive thinking, for finally our headlights picked out these two white abodes and we wearily lifted out our bags and stumbling in the darkness were shown into one of them.

Here by the light of the one dim hanging paraffin lamp, we all squeezed in making our apologies to the elderly lady already tucked up in the single iron-framed bed. The face of a small child sharing the bed with her peeked out with wide-eyed curiosity at these strange-looking people.

The floor in this yurt was to be our bedroom for the night, and we were all so exhausted, just to know that we were only moments away from sleep was a great relief and this overruled any other thoughts that might have presented themselves had we been shown this accommodation in a normal situation.

The temperature had dropped dramatically once the sun had disappeared and it was now distinctly cold as we rolled out our sleeping bags on the floor ready to jump into them.

My companions donned leggings to add to their night attire and there was much amusement among them when I pulled out my white satin nightdress.

Strangely the need to sleep in this clothing had come over ten years previously and coincided with the 'Spiritual Emergency', the event which had instantaneously and dramatically changed my beliefs and every part of my life in so many ways.

No way! Not even here on the floor of a yurt in the vast expanse of Siberia could I pass the night in anything else!

After only a few short hours of sleep morning dawned. I opened my eyes and noticed that the two occupants of the bed were already up and gone.

We were in such close proximity that the act of waking up seemed to spread like a virus and within minutes we were all starting to move. Someone opened the door and I raised myself up a little to look out.

We seemed to be in the middle of nowhere for there was an endless stretch of barren land, all one color, just varying shades of khaki. There was not one tree or shrub, not a hill or rock, neither man nor beast. This uninterrupted view went so far that one expected to see the earth start to curve.

I reached out and pulled on my long coat that I had used as additional bedcovering and slipping my feet into my boots stepped outside.

Sam and Jennifer joined me and we all took a deep breath and filled our lungs with the clean fresh air. As we looked around we were relieved to find we were not in isolation for there were signs of activity on both sides and also behind our sleeping quarters.

There were small pens of sheep and goats all standing quietly with heads down eating who only gave us a cursory return glance, a few horses were tethered nearby and the family they belonged to were at this moment attending to them. On the far side of the pens there stood another yurt from which the Tuvan shamans were also emerging and we gave them a wave.

The response from Sam to Jennifer, when she was asked, "Where do you think the bathroom is?" was, "Anywhere you want it to be."

This journey was really going to be a 'back to basics' one.

It is refreshing to see how adaptable people find they can become when the circumstances necessitate. And some hundred yards away from the yurts we found a small stream through which a trickle of water was still running, although it was narrow and at present little more than a trench. The sharpness of the banks showed how high the water usually ran.

With bottled water to scrub our teeth and this other source to cleanse the rest of us, we managed to complete our ablutions.

Returning to the yurt we found our hostess, a tiny lady with a smile shining out from a face of a thousand wrinkles, busy stoking up the stove and sitting on it was a flask of hot milky tea. She reached out to grasp my hand and the strength of her clasp defied her aged appearance.

This grandmother and I had lives that ran parallel. I knew they would be so similar in many ways, yet to a casual observer they would seem worlds apart.

Out here on the Steppes she was the matriarch of the family, the cook preparing the meals and the hub around which the family's well-being, both physical and spiritual, revolved. To complete the picture a small grandchild was hanging onto her skirt for security, but shyly peeping at us.

Today this lady had an additional seven guests for breakfast, whose belongings were spread over her living room floor. The magnitude of this Tuvan lady was revealed as, without words, she just looked around at this motley group in her home and with a huge smile embraced us all.

After eating a large bowl of hot porridge-like cereal, we quickly packed up our belongings, once more picked up our bags and along with all the shamans climbed back onto the coach and into the vans, and our convoy set off for what we were told was a one-hour trip to the village of Berdag.

This place we were told was the home of Heurell, who we also now learned was the brother-in-law of Moon Heart.

This comparatively short drive was bumpy but uneventful, with no stops and with the scenery a continuation of the expansive tundra. That is, until we spotted we were drawing ever closer to a small range of mountains, but not the high snow-covered ones we had become familiar with. These were bare and of a darkish brown while at their base was an expanse of woodland.

This was our destination and when we reached the edge of the trees we pulled into a wooden-housed community of about 30–40 dwellings, each with a small fenced-off garden. As we stopped, a small pack of barking dogs ran out to signal our arrival and mark their territory.

Trying to ignore the sniffing dogs at our heels we followed

Heurell, who firmly shut the garden gate on them before showing us into his home, where we were introduced to and warmly welcomed by his wife. The seven of us, plus Galena and Rollanda, were shown into the tiny sitting room of this very small house and invited to sit down. There were only a couple of chairs but cushions were found and most of us sat on the floor. Within minutes canned drinks were offered and then about thirty minutes later food was lavished on us. All the while we bombarded Rollanda with questions, lots of them practical. We wondered how these people, living so far away from the town, managed during the times when severe weather would render them housebound.

Once we had finished eating, Heurell's wife proudly allowed us to view her larder, which was such a surprise for she started by rolling back the small carpet we were sitting on to reveal a trapdoor.

She lifted the wooden cover and we peered in. A short ladder led down to a depth of about six feet into a small cellar, really no more than a hole in the ground, which was about four feet square, and here were stored sacks of carrots and beets, dried fruit, currants and mushrooms all gathered from the surrounding taiga, and a good supply of the self-ground wheat for their bread making.

My thoughts flashed back to the cellar built for this same purpose that had sat beneath the grand old manor house that I had lived in for twenty years of my life. This had been ten times the size, with huge marble shelves, grilled windows and a brick floor with special drains. What I was looking at was literally a hole in the ground where Mother Nature with her perma-frozen ground did the caring for these precious possessions perfectly well and held them in the heart of the home.

A group of children, who I assumed were the children of our hosts and their friends, with their wind-burnished red faces, stood in the doorway of this room gazing with fascination at this motley group of strangers invading their sanctuary. One of them came into the room, and looking up at Heurell appeared to ask him a question which brought forth a burst of laughter. We looked towards Rollanda and we saw she too was much amused.

"What did he say?" asked Sam.

Rollanda paused for a second before sharing the joke.

"You must realize," she said, "he has never seen people from outside his village before. What he said was... 'These people are all different colors just like our horses.'"

We loved this description; it was another innocent remark that became a memory to treasure.

We had all eaten well and after this show of typical Tuvan hospitality we were guided to another building. As we passed through the freshly-painted doors we saw that here all the other shamans traveling with us had gathered.

This newly decorated building was where Heurell was in the process of opening a Shamanic Clinic, one to be run on the same lines as that in Kyzyl. A place where the shamans could practice their skills and those suffering either physical or emotional problems could seek help.

This small house had been purchased and paid for with the money his sister-in law was now earning on her trips to Italy and was to be the village focal point, a center where the community and the outlying small family units could gather and once again practice their age-old healing techniques and affirm their beliefs in the powers of the spirits. These long-held beliefs that neither Christianity nor Communism were able to dislodge.

The clinic at present, although clean and smart, was totally devoid of furniture, so everyone sat down on the floor. Moon Heart was going to speak to us; we were eager pupils, ready to learn and slowly these people opened up to us. They began to share some of their age-old wisdom and gave us a glimpse into secrets that our culture had lost eons ago.

During this time Heurell spoke to us about the importance of the drum. His words held a reverence that awoke in us a new respect for this most ancient and sacred instrument. He instructed us in the care of our drums, how they should be laid when not in use and reminded us to greet our drums each new day, to remember to feed them by rolling bread around the inside and occasionally rubbing butter over the skin.

He instilled in us the awareness that through drumming it is possible to mentally journey anywhere and our drum will always lead us where we want or need to go. It will take us to magical places where the two worlds, the material and the spiritual, meet; places where we can communicate with the ancestors, to seek help and guidance from them and thus continue with the difficult and often fraught lives we lead with added assistance from these sources.

Nadia also offered an insight into their ways with us by sharing some of the tribal wisdom that has been accumulated over many years. Tuvans spend many hours talking and sharing stories; it's a wonderful way to pass the long dark days of winter. Her role as a shaman is also very much that of a counselor member of the community; others will come to her with problems that people the world over have to face. Continually within a small village there are personality conflicts, misunderstandings in a relationship, willful children and a constant battle to merely survive.

Here her approach to the problems differs to that in our culture for she incorporates even the planetary movements in her search to aid the client in discovering a solution.

She may even advise them to come back in perhaps two weeks before she will begin to help, because dependent on the problem, the moon needs to be at a specific phase for the maximum help to be obtained.

Seeds are planted at a certain time of the year, not necessarily at the first sign of spring, and the herbs used for ailments will also be picked and prepared at an auspicious time.

We were also reminded by Nadia of a basic premise for she recommended that we take our time with a patient, to sit quietly with them before any form of healing is commenced. To look closely at their energy field and to set store by what we FEEL, what the sensitive part of our being is reporting.

Our shaman friends even found a Russian surgeon who happened to be visiting friends in the village who spoke with us.

This lady, who practiced in one of Moscow's hospitals, shared with us a wonderful story.

She told how orthodox medicine had been unable to resolve a long-standing medical problem she had been suffering with; however, last year after just one visit to a shaman she had had no recurrence and considered herself cured.

She felt a powerful empathy with the Red Rock Mountains that overlook this village and felt the energy from this natural source had played an important part in the healing process.

This was an incident that showed how the freedom of individuals in this country is rapidly growing. To share admission of these beliefs a short time ago would have put her career in jeopardy as well as endangering the very lives of the shamans who were prepared to help her.

Each of the other shamans shared a little of their knowledge, but when Llyn said, "We would be very interested to watch you work. Perhaps one of you would do a healing ceremony on one of us?" this request was sidestepped.

Time moved on towards late afternoon and once again, as they had yesterday, they asked us to treat some of the villagers and once again, in spite of our insistence that we were the ones wishing to learn from them, we found we were unable to refuse.

Llyn who had visited this area on the previous year led us to a beautiful spot in the nearby woodland. It was very close to a river where although the level was low, the sparkling water ran swift and clear. From here away in the distance we could also see the tops of the Red Rock Mountains.

In a small clearing, which we first tidied by pulling to one side some small logs and dead branches, we carefully wafted the smoke from some tobacco-stuffed pipes and did a little drumming. We also cleansed the area before we sat quietly in a circle for a short meditation and requested help and guidance from the spirits with the task that lay ahead.

As we concluded this final preparation the shamans, both of our interpreters and a small group of villagers arrived.

The shamans sat down in a row on a fallen tree, looking like a lineup of judges and the assortment of both men and women from the village stood in silence, their faces totally impassive.

Gisela again wanted to work individually, and the moment Rollanda translated her wishes three of the people immediately stepped forward. Leading one of them by the hand, Gisela walked off into the woodland telling Rollanda she would work on all three, but only one at a time.

I had been feeling a little uncomfortable during the preparing of the site, not ill or even remotely unwell, but suddenly this feeling intensified.

I didn't want to be part of this. I felt drawn to go and sit down on the log alongside the shamans. The voice in my head was almost shouting at me, ordering me: "Go and sit down with them!"

But I battled with it and refused to follow this demand from an unseen source.

However, as Mike and Llyn and then Jennifer were paired up with a patient I seemed unable to remain and quickly turned on my heel and left the clearing. I walked deeper into the woods and then followed the river as it ran, staying close to the bank to ensure I didn't get lost. I found a spot where there was a break in the trees that gave a clear view of the mountains, and here I sat for over an hour.

Finally I got to my feet, found my way back to the clearing and stood for a while watching Jennifer using the same healing techniques that the shamans living in Ortovalo had taught her.

I looked around at the scene. The Tuvan shamans were still sitting on the fallen tree closely observing the proceedings, occasionally turning and making a comment to one another. Sam and Llyn were working together on a young man a short distance away and there was no sign of either Mike or Gisela.

There was now an even larger group of the villagers silently waiting, but I felt totally unmoved and detached from all the activity, and after a few minutes I again left this site and walked back towards the houses. The bus was still parked where it had pulled in when we arrived and my feet led me towards it.

I looked up at the windscreen.

The carving of the Maha Kala that I had left there was missing!

My stomach turned over... the panic I felt at seeing it missing was out of proportion.

I turned around, but the place was silent and deserted; everyone was down in the woods where the healings were taking place. But at that moment the gate leading from Heurell's home opened and he walked out.

Somehow with a lot of gesticulation and repeating the words, "Missing, missing, gone!", and pointing to the place in the window where everyone had observed and remarked on this dramatic carving, I saw an understanding cross his face.

Putting up his hand to indicate to me to remain where I was he turned and hurriedly walked up a narrow pathway between his house and the next one.

I stood there in the silent and deserted village, feeling on the verge of tears. Suddenly this carved image of the Maha Kala had taken on a value totally unrelated to its financial cost and I had a profound sense of its spiritual importance for me.

It felt an age, but was probably only a few minutes, before Heurell returned emerging from the side of the high fence with this precious image in his hands. He bowed slightly as with both hands he held out the carving and presented it to me rather than just returning it.

As I once more held it, an enormous sense of relief washed over me and I vowed from now on to keep it close to me.

Slowly I retraced my footsteps back to the clearing and sat down at the edge to watch the proceedings. A couple of children who were probably about seven or eight years old shyly came over and stood looking at me. I lifted up my hand and beckoned to them to sit down next to me. They both hesitated, yet remained staring intently at me.

The energy here was totally different from the village where we had done the healing work yesterday, but it seemed my companions had been getting some very good results and word had spread like wildfire. There was no shortage of patients and a queue had formed.

Rollanda spotted me and came across. "Wendy. We need you to do a healing," she said. But I shook my head and said, "Sorry. No."

As a schoolteacher she was very persuasive, but I was adamant.

I could not offer her a reason why, but knew I had to follow this instinctive feeling and she finally accepted defeat and gave up.

I remained seated, just silently watching, still clutching to my chest the image of the Tibetan deity. A short while after this encounter I watched as Llyn firmly told her, "No more!" As the leader she had a responsibility to contain her own energy and was well aware that we were still at the beginning of an arduous journey. It was with much relief that Sam and Jennifer agreed that they too could do no more.

Mike and Gisela alone elected to continue a little while longer. In the event it was another hour before they called a halt, and came across to join the rest of us who had been sitting relaxing and resting, sharing water and snacks from our backpacks.

But the moment the final healing was complete Rollanda immediately led us away from the wooded area informing us that we were about to take part in another ceremony and Gisela and Mike were given no chance to even sit down for five minutes. We picked up our drums and bags and walked out of the woods and around the small group of houses to the other side of the village, where as we turned the corner we saw we were at the base of a small barren hill.

Rollanda pointed up to the top. "The ceremony will take place up there," she said. "Moon Heart is waiting for you."

We puffed our way as we slowly progressed up the steep side, finally reaching the top and as we crossed the ridge we saw a very large ovaa.

This site was obviously in constant use for the pile of stones here was the largest we had yet seen. In the center stood a strong mast with a rigging of several ropes that ran from the top out to the base; the tattered cloths attached to them holding the dreams and prayers of the community fluttering about in a strong wind.

Moon Heart stood by the side of it; she was now in her ceremonial robes which were blowing in harmony with the colored streamers.

Common language was unnecessary as she used just her hands to instruct us to place our drums at the edge of the ovaa and to indicate that each of us was then to collect nine large stones and add them to this structure.

This task took a while as over the years petitioners had cleared the area closest to the ovaa of any worthwhile rocks and we had to search further afield to find, carry and then make our contribution.

On the top of this hill were also several circles of about a 12 foot diameter marked out by stones. These we had to circle three times in a right-handed direction; no reason was given and we completed this task without question.

A stack of wood also indicated that another fire ceremony lay ahead and this was by the side of yet another marked-out circle, the center of which showed it would not be the first time a fire had been lit atop this hill.

While we had been performing these tasks under the guidance of Natasha, I saw that our shamans were in a heated argument with a group of villagers and I wondered what it was all about. Later I would learn that there was considerable dissension between two groups in this village, those that favored the return to shamanism and another section who were staunch Buddhists.

I had no idea Buddhism was an ideology now practiced in Tuva. This greatly surprised me. Even more than that it brought me down to earth in the recognition of the frailties of human nature that these people should argue over the use of this piece of land for spiritual practice... Both beliefs were surely just two different ways up the same mountain!

A short while later Rollanda made her way up and joined us. She informed us that this forthcoming ceremony would incorporate a blessing for our new drums and told us to now move our drums from where they sat at the base of the ovaa and had according to her been absorbing the energy of these stones, and to lean them against the outside perimeter of the protective stones of the fire area.

With shamanic ceremony all over the world, with every culture there is always a lot of waiting, a lot of discussion, a lot of sitting around all amid a general air that there is nothing happening. All so far removed from the Western church service that starts promptly at a previously agreed time.

With these people who conduct their lives in tune with the rhythms of the earth, of the spirits and the ancestors, the time to commence is when everything falls into place and they sense the time is right; then suddenly everything happens and the whole scene springs to life.

We stood around. It was very late; the sun was close to setting and the light dimming when the action finally began.

Earlier we had watched Heurell reverently and methodically stack the large sticks, and now he came forward from the ring of shamans standing around him in a circle and the fire was lit.

First there must be fire, for the Tuvans believe it is through fire that all the gods and spirits are reached. The center of our earth is fire and the sun that shines down on us is a ball of fire. Fire is the spirit that lives within us.

It was a dramatic scene, for with the setting of the sun a wind had blown up and here at the top of an exposed hill this caught the flames and danced with them before sweeping them skywards.

We stood transfixed as the wind increased and the flames from the fire bent sideways, then flared and changed direction. The shamans drummed and swirled, reflected in the red light of the fire; the wind lifting the feathers of their robes and at times there came an expectation that they would lift off from the ground and fly.

The stars now were lighting the dark night sky and the power of the ceremony was tangible. Our drums sat by the stones in this most powerful setting and were imbued with the essence of this night.

More wood was added to the fire and then we were invited to pick up our drums and join with the ecstatic beat of the shamans.

The place, ceremony, the fire, the sound and the visual effects together produced a power and energy, and in spite of a long and exhausting day we drummed with a vigor that surprised us all.

Finally we sensed the slowing down that indicated the ceremony was coming to an end, and one by one we lowered our beaters, placed our drums on the ground and got to our knees before finally resting our foreheads on the earth.

This event produced a memorable closure to a long day and we stumbled down the hill in the darkness aided only by the light of the moon.

In silence we climbed back into the bus and for a further hour bumped over the rough roads all the way back to our temporary home.

Here we again spent the night within the confines of the yurt, but very happy to do so. Tonight the iron bedstead was empty. Galena assured us the grandmother and child were already asleep in the other yurt.

It was impossible to imagine where, but it was ridiculous to waste the extra space we now had and we persuaded Mike as the largest person to shift his sleeping bag on to it and the other seven of us again arranged ourselves on the floor around the central stove.

It was cramped, but it worked! I was just so happy to be here and I felt enveloped in a sense of 'returning', a feeling that strengthened my belief in reincarnation.

I fell into a dreamless sleep; maybe my head was too full of the day's experiences to cope with any more or maybe it was just too tired to initiate any recall.

Chapter 7

In the morning we said good-bye to this hospitable family and to this area of Tuva for we were setting off to travel deeper into the Steppe, and these nomads who had opened their homes and hearts to us were also moving on to find fresh grazing for their animals.

I felt such empathy with the aged grandmother who had been our hostess. We were traveling light and apart from a few small items, like a packet of balloons and a couple of little bubble blowing pots for the children, I had brought no gifts, so I gave her the jacket I was wearing. It was no big deal for I had a spare lightweight one in my bag and knew I could always layer up with jumpers (sweaters) if needed.

In return she rewarded me with a delighted smile which was a greater gift for me, one I could carry everywhere. I could hold in my heart the picture of her going about her day on the Siberian Steppe cherishing a worn garment that had come with me from the South of England.

These people are so respectful of our planet that when they departed the only trace that would reveal numerous people had dwelt here in this small spot for many days would be the darkened circles on the land where the two yurts had stood, and with a drop of rain these small areas would heal in a matter of days.

As we were putting our bags into the coach, I saw Llyn standing with a concerned look on her face. "Is anything wrong?" I asked.

"It's Gisela," she admitted. "She's being very discreet. But she is not at all well. She's been throwing up most of the night. We've a tough journey ahead and that will turn into a nightmare for anyone feeling ill."

She gave a big sigh. "There is no choice. We must leave now."

Our transport from this point onwards for us and all the shamans was to be in four-wheel drive vehicles. We would be traversing the almost uninhabited southern region of the Sayan Mountains.

Most of our belongings were deposited in the coach and would remain there until we returned. Now, and with just a minimal bag of clothing and a few personal necessities, we headed off packed into one of three of these vehicles.

We appeared to have been given the best of these ancient Russian rejects, because when she saw that we had an unoccupied seat Ai-Churek chose to join us. In the rest of the jeeps there were more passengers than seats so some of the shamans were sitting on the floor. Each jeep had come with a driver and also a spare mechanic/driver; this was a sure sign that ahead of us lay what was going to be an arduous trip, a journey unlike any other.

The first few hours were along a reasonable road, but it was almost deserted, the landscape showed no sign of habitation and we saw just an occasional vehicle going in the opposite direction.

We then turned off this thoroughfare and bounced along a dirt track where the jeeps took turns leading as the dust thrown up was thick and choking. The heat was almost unbearable and sometimes I almost forgot we were in Siberia!

It amazed us to discover after a period of considerable bone-jarring distance that we had arrived at a small village, a place so far from what the rest of us refer to as 'civilization'. We learned that a group of over one hundred people lived here, people who had to be totally self-sustainable.

This village was called U-Shina and was composed of the familiar wooden build single-floor dwelling, with one door and just a couple of windows and again each building was enclosed by a substantial picket fence.

I failed to ask why each small dirt yard needed to be contained as the children and dogs ran freely from one home to the next in the warm sunshine. Later it occurred to me that maybe in the depths of winter they were protection from packs of marauding hungry wolves!

There was little to differentiate one house from another; all were approximately the same size and ran on either side in a straight line down just the one street. We drew up outside what was the largest building in this settlement. It was almost like two put close enough together to have an interior connecting door. This proved to be the community center and here already waiting our arrival was a welcoming committee.

For Gisela it was a great relief to simply be stationary. Her condition had deteriorated rapidly during the journey, and she found great difficulty in holding herself upright. All she wanted to do was lie down.

The rest of us alighted from the cramped conditions of our transport, dusty and disheveled, and stood looking like a group of tramps.

Immediately the head of the village stepped forward to greet us. He was smartly dressed in what was a very 'dated' but well-preserved suit, and stood proudly before us as he gave a well-rehearsed speech of welcome. Rollanda's interpretation ran close to his words and they invoked in us a sense of humility, for he told us how the people of this place had been looking forward to our visit for many weeks. They considered it an honor for them that we should be accompanying their shamans and participating in these important Tuvan rituals.

He was flanked by seven young girls, who with their high cheekbones, large eyes and jet-black hair were all stunning in their looks. As if their beauty were not enough to enrich the eyes, they were all wearing the traditional Tuvan gowns. In blues, reds and gold the sunlight shimmered on the satin material that made up these full-length, high-necked gowns. Completing the outfits were little silver hats worn with an upturned brim, trimmed with beads, and adding to the effect and eye catching as they moved were long beaded earrings.

They stood behind this spokesman of the village, no doubt as bemused by our appearance as we were entranced by theirs.

Once the speech was over and we had been given a deep bow to which we all likewise responded, the girls moved forward and gently placed a Khata scarf around the neck of each one of us, the same material and pattern of our previous gifts but this time in a beautiful peacock blue color. This ceremony was followed by the handing out again of a delicate porcelain drinking bowl into which they poured sweet hot tea for us to drink and once again Rollanda told us these items were gifts for us to take home.

While we were being feted Gisela had remained in the jeep, for with it now empty she had spread her long body out on the floor and was feeling too unwell to even move.

Now we were invited to step into the building and from a small double door lobby we entered a room that was almost filled by a large table laid ready for a meal.

Three jovial Tuvan men came into the room and signaled for us to sit down. I presumed they were elders of the village, and another feast had been prepared for us as they went in and out several times bringing back full-assorted platefuls of food. In front of us they placed a meal fit for a king before sitting to join us.

The main dish held the cooked shoulder blade of a sheep and I listened as Rollanda said, "This is the very best part of the animal," and added, "It is only served to the most important guests. They will honor you by cutting a slice and offering it on the point of a knife. Please accept this honor by taking it. To refuse would cause them pain."

For over twenty years it had been my choice to maintain a strict vegetarian diet, and for a brief moment I felt turmoil and my throat and stomach muscles contracted, but there comes a time when even the most rigid rules we impose on ourselves need to be overturned and this was one of them.

These people I knew had much to teach me; in order to learn I needed to immerse myself in their culture. My Western habits and beliefs had to remain for the time being at home.

I accepted the offering and was so happy I did as a few minutes later one of my companions refused the meat and I saw the flash of pain that crossed our host's face.

Now the Universe had presented me with another lesson, I knew I needed to accept her decision and allow it to pass and make sure no anger or shame for her actions remained attached to my memories of this incident.

Our hosts waited on us until they were satisfied we were truly full up and needed nothing more. Then they left the room and Rollanda and Llyn stood up and followed, leaving the rest of us with sweet cakes and hot tea to relax for a little while.

I fingered the silk scarf that still hung around my neck. This was the second time on this trip that we had been gifted these scarves, which I knew were traditionally exchanged in Tibet, but I had not expected to find them here in Tuva. Now as I sat in this isolated place surrounded by the timelessness of the mountains and the vast tundra I pondered the connection.

In our short time here in this country I had already recognized that the people we were meeting had great integrity. These scarves were symbolic items that they treated with great respect, knowing what they symbolized.

About ten minutes later, the door opened and Llyn and Rollanda came back in, both looking a little concerned.

"We are going to have to wait for a while before we continue," said Llyn. "I know we are surrounded by shamans, but I have also asked if the village doctor will attend to Gisela. She is really ill. Once we leave here there will be no contact with anyone and I want to be on the safe side and take advantage of all the help that is available."

Llyn, as the organizer and leader of this expedition, was carrying a huge responsibility and she asked that we all remain in the building for the time being. The thought of even one of us going off for a walk would add to her stress load and at present this was something she wished to avoid.

I took the opportunity of this confinement to share a personal story with my friends regarding an incident that had taken place some two years previously when I had been blessed to meet with His Holiness the Dalai Lama, while traveling through Ladakh, and had been personally given a Khata scarf by him.

This gift had been surrounded by a series of synchronistic and mysterious events and had proven to be imbued with powerful healing energies.

It was strange to be sitting here in Siberia, sharing this story with my American friends, for the fascinating tale that I had just related had so many links. It had originated in Ireland, then connected India and England before arriving here, but somehow it provided a link and it tuned us into the unity of everything that exists in the Universe.

So much of our time during this trip through Siberia had been focused on the healing forces and I had a feeling that I was once again playing the role of messenger. Only time would tell in which way I was to be used, but I was a willing participant.

Galena went in search of Rollanda and Llyn, returning a short while later to give us an update on the situation with Gisela and the ongoing plan.

We also learned from her that this very day had, many weeks ago, been designated as the right time to re-consecrate the local ovaa which was sited a few miles away, for this day was the eve of the Summer Solstice and a most auspicious day.

For many years the site of this ovaa, even in such a remote area, had been neglected and ignored due to fears of reprisal during the Communist reign, but now it was coming back into use by the elders and had once again become a focal point for the prayers and offerings of the local people.

Here, even the younger residents were showing an interest in this site, a place which the older Tuvans living in the area claim as a place of special energy.

We learned that they considered this place an area where the divide between our world and that of the spirits was at its thinnest, a place where communication between the two worlds was easier to achieve; it was a spot recognized as an inter-dimensional portal.

U-Shina was another community also becoming increasingly worried at the absence of rain, and many weeks ago, when the concern at the lack of this natural and necessary element started to seriously grow, it was decided to add in an additional ritual to honor the rain spirits to the re-consecrating ceremony.

The village doctor had by now visited Gisela. This happened to be a lady who had trained and worked in Moscow and had now returned to live back in her community, bringing with her this newly-gained knowledge to add to the traditional methods. She typified this new belief in holistic medicine that surely must be to the benefit of all of us and an additional aid and comfort for the sick in this remote place.

We all climbed back into the jeep and poor Gisela had no option but to sit upright. She did this uncomplainingly and endured what was an uncomfortable one hour ride, and which for her must have been nightmarish.

It was with some apprehension that we realized Mike was also becoming unwell.

In the West, if you are going to be sick, you are never far from a doctor or hospital. Here in the middle of nowhere, traveling with a group of shamans had to be quite fortuitous. However, I could see that Llyn was deeply concerned, for we were traveling ever deeper into the Steppes. She has, however, an incredible faith that we are all in the right place at the right time, a philosophy that I heartily endorse, but as group facilitator this belief was being well tested.

The distance to the sacred site as the crow flies was probably short but our drive was over very rough terrain and took over an hour. We were accompanied by what seemed the whole of the village as an assortment of ancient vehicles weighed down with bodies took us on this hazardous track into the foothills of the mountains.

Incorporated into the planned ceremony, Rollanda told us, there would also be a ritual to the water spirits, a heartfelt request for some rain to fall on this isolated spot and answer the prayers of these people.

It must have been a great relief to both Gisela and Mike when we finally arrived at the base of yet another hill and stopped. As I looked around I saw we were still surrounded by even more towering tops; however, atop this one I could see stood the now familiar stack of stones, with the upright post in the center holding the strings of the fluttering votive rags and ribbons.

We were like an army of ants as the vehicles disgorged passengers and we started our upward climb.

The young helped the elderly up the steppe slope; there were mothers carrying babies and fathers assisting the toddlers. All work had been abandoned for the rest of the day; this was a community event with a festive atmosphere and all wished to participate.

Gradually everyone succeeded in reaching the top, and the villagers arranged themselves seated in a large circle a short distance away from the ovaa, and where a patch in the center held the telltale burnt sign of earlier bonfires.

As wood that had been brought with us was shared out, carried up and placed close to the ashes, Heurell took over and began to ceremonially stack the nine layers and near the hill to the jeep we were again instructed to each collect nine stones to add to the ovaa pile. Our group participated in this ritual with the exception of Gisela, who took advantage of the empty jeep and lay down again. To make sure her presence was included, Jennifer and I between us gathered an extra nine stones as an offering on her behalf and added them along with the contribution from everyone else.

As I placed the last of my stones in position, I straightened up and took a few minutes to stand and gaze at my surroundings. Maybe some would have described this scene as colorless, but I found it quite beautiful. The hills and valleys were varying shades of burnished brown with rocks that appeared white where the sun was striking them, but a few feet away those in the shade looked almost black. I tipped my head and looked up into the sky and there right above our heads were three eagles soaring on the thermals and every so often swooping down for a closer look at the proceedings.

What a magical sight and this I felt added an extra power to the preparations.

Ai-Churek, I was rapidly discovering, has a personal relationship with the spirits, and I was sure the ceremony that was about to commence would be just the visual part, the icing on the cake but so much more would once again remain unseen.

This woman spends hours in solitude and meditation communing with the elements of our planet, and she is constantly engaged in private ritual maintaining her rapport with the spirits and the ancestors.

I heard the call that went out for us all to gather and form a circle with the Tuvan shamans. We hurriedly went down the hill to the jeep, and after retrieving our drums and Khata scarves from the van, puffed our way back to the top and joined the others who had already changed into their colorful robes. Now this multinational little group made a smaller circle between the seated villagers and where Heurell was kneeling ready to put the first match to the wood.

Prior to the first drumbeat being sounded, Ai-Churek honored the elementals of the four directions by saluting them one by one and throwing bread and milk up into the air. She also made offerings to the sky and then to the earth by saluting them in the same manner.

Heurell had by now put a lighted match to the fire and the flames began to rise, then like an open mouth it devoured the handful of grain that Ai-Churek threw into them.

Her voice as she performs these actions is in constant use and I am sure there are many small rituals she performs that pass unnoticed by the uninitiated.

But of one thing I am sure, the force she generates is immense; she is awesome to witness for the air becomes electric with the energy and power at her command.

Today as the ceremony got under way and the sound of drumming echoed around the mountains it was met with the response of a rumble of thunder.

An hour later it was all over and Llyn and Rollanda tried hard to get us all loaded back into the van but the villagers were reluctant to let us leave, and they all wished to shake each one of us by the hand and to thank us individually.

We fervently hoped that their confidence in this ceremony to promote some heavy precipitation would be fulfilled.

From this point onwards our journey was totally dependent on the reliability of our vehicle and the skills of our drivers to effect any necessary repairs. Both were tested frequently as the terrain grew increasingly rougher. Several times the gradient took on the steepest of angles and we got out to ease the load and walked on the rock-strewn track.

Once when the steep track circumnavigated the side of a mountain the width of the path was only fractionally larger than the wheelbase of the jeeps. Here again Rollanda asked us to get out and walk and this time she instructed us to take our passports with us.

It was a strange request, but we learned that there was a very real fear that the vehicle might go over the edge and we watched the lone driver take his life in his hands as he guided the wheels along this hazardous trail.

Even Gisela had to get out and walk at this point, which she did without complaint, but we could see the effort it was requiring, for her pallor was grey and she was breathing heavily. Mike also had to make several stops to sit and rest and we walked at the pace of the slowest which made it reasonably easy for the rest of us.

Soon all connection to time was lost. We traversed one mountain and then there was another. As we reached each summit, the sky seemed to extend forever; we saw no sign of habitation whatsoever.

Finally as we stood atop yet another one, we saw that we were now at the end of this ridge, for lying out below us were tundra and plains that stretched unbroken to the lands of Mongolia. Here the sky was vast and still a cloudless blue, but we were coming to the end of the day, imperceptibly the temperature was dropping and we began to remove our spare clothes from our bags, and in an attempt to keep warm added them to what we were already wearing as another layer.

Tomorrow would be Midsummer's Day. This was the night of the Summer Solstice and we knew that we would be up all night participating in a ceremony on one of the most important days of the year. Finally we reached our destination, a level area where there continued to be an unrestricted 360 degree view; now we were only 30 miles from the Mongolian border.

As we stepped down from the vans we looked out from this plateau in silence; to try and find words to describe it would do it an injustice.

The sky, the mountains, the trees and the land, the power of the place touched us all.

There is a shamanic belief that mountains are especially sacred because they are closest to the heavens. This spot was several thousand feet high, and although in the overall scheme of things there are many mountains far larger, this in no way diminished its energy and somehow I understood what the shamans meant.

On the brow as we had entered this plateau stood a sacred tree. This short and squat fir tree had been pointed out to us as something special. The format of this tree was unique for it had a normal single main trunk but shooting out from the roots and growing in a circle around it were nine smaller trees. It was the sacred number nine, and once again this fir tree with its offshoots were the only species of this kind in the area.

From a distance it was difficult to see any of the greenery such was the extent of the decorative rags that adorned it. This provoked even more amazement because our journey here had been long and hazardous. It would be an arduous pilgrimage without vehicles just to reach this remote site, but here were signs of the many people that made the effort to do just this.

This tree was an icon for the Tuvans, and we learned that they treated it with a reverence that surpassed all that had been offered in the earlier ceremonies.

Rollanda gathered us together as we emerged from the jeep, before we could walk off to stretch our legs.

"Your first duty," she said, "is to go three times around the tree, in a sun-wise direction. But not," she added, "walking. For this tree you must do it on your knees."

Constantly I was being given reminders of how these people immerse themselves in the natural world. We use the word 'clockwise'; here I was learning they use the word 'sun-wise', a small indication of the difference in our attitudes.

Gisela had remained in the jeep and as I looked around I saw that Mike also had not felt well enough to get out.

The other five of us that now comprised our group stood there unmoving, checking to see if our interpreter was serious, for the ground here on the top of the mountain was hard and stony. We glanced towards the tree; already Ai-Churek was on her knees in the process of doing just that, so on the rough ground with the sharp flints cutting into the skin of our soft knees we all duly completed our rotations crawling three times around its base, which with the nine offshoots made the overall circumference a fair distance.

This pilgrimage was completed by placing our foreheads to the ground and spending a few minutes in silent prayer.

The Tuvan women first focused on our physical needs, our drivers soon had a regular fire lit and before long mugs of sweet tea, hot soup and bread was being shared around. There was little conversation; a combination of the exhaustion of the day's events and the knowledge that we had to keep awake for many more hours kept us silent and in our own thoughts.

The comparatively flat level on top of this mountain extended a few hundred yards, but we were asked to remain beside this fire until we were called. The light had suddenly faded and with the day gone a bitter night wind had blown up, so we were happy to follow these instructions.

Gisela and Mike were still continuing to feel unwell; Llyn said both were running high temperatures and they wished to remain in the van.

It may be just a 'tummy bug', I thought, but I also wondered if the energy they had expended by doing so many healings on the residents of U-Shina had been the cause of their exhaustion.

Whatever it was I just hoped for their sakes that they would make a rapid recovery.

The Tuvan shamans had moved a short distance away and we could see their outline as they started a second fire and heard them as they began the ritualistic throwing of offerings to the spirits in preparation for the coming ceremony marking the Summer Solstice.

As night took over from day the temperature dropped even further and the cold began to eat into us, but the beauty of the sky more than compensated. A million stars with a brightness unseen in our light-polluted lands arrived for us to feast our eyes upon.

As I gazed upwards I heard the first beats of the shamans' drums and at that same moment a shooting star sped across the sky.

This is a moment we so rarely witness and to have it coincide with that drumbeat gave a powerful start to the proceedings; I was discovering personally how the vibration of drumming attunes you to everything.

We remained physically separate from the other group for another ten minutes, but sat silently immersing ourselves in the sound. Then Rollanda passed the message, "It is time for you to join the shamans. Come to the other fire, bring your drums and when you are ready you may start beating and join in with the shamans."

"Just wait a moment while I check on Mike and Gisela," Llyn said.

A few moments later she was back. "Gisela is staying where she is, but Mike wants to join us. Between us we can help him over there and get him back in his sleeping bag. He feels it would help him to be part of the circle and I agree."

Leaving just our drivers to sit enjoying the warmth coming from this fire we went to the van and between us all we half carried Mike and did all we could to try and make him comfortable. In a space quite close to the fire we cleared the largest of the rocks, laid out his Therm-a-Rest and his sleeping bag. Then like five handmaidens waiting on him and to the accompaniment of the shamans who sat around continuing to softly drum, we removed his boots and helped him slide down into his bag.

The effort had exhausted him and the only response to the enquiry regarding his comfort was a murmured, "Hmmm."

Then each of us found a spot to sit among the loose rock and flint that covered the surface of this mountaintop. Reaching under our bottoms to remove the sharpest of the stones, tightening down our hoods and ensuring the zips on our jackets were pulled up, we prepared for a marathon.

For a while I left my drum on the ground in front of me and sat allowing the power of the place to seep into me and then I leaned forward and, with slow deliberation, picked up my drum with both hands before I allowed my right hand to retrieve the beater and then softly at first I joined in.

We followed their lead as the drumming from the shamans continued nonstop. It came in waves; sometimes it sped up, and the tempo increased and got louder and was accompanied by vocal calls from them that rang out into the clear night sky. Sometimes, without any apparent signal, it would slow and for a brief moment go down to almost a whisper but at no time did it stop and at no time was there silence from the beat on skin.

Somehow the tiredness vanished; occasionally a wave of fatigue would pass through me and I would take a break for a few short moments until this wave quickly vanished into the darkness and I would resume the beating.

Occasionally in the darkness I could tell from the sound that the Tuvan shamans were those drumming while we from the West took a break, then the roles were reversed and purely from the vibration and sound I knew that our hosts were briefly resting.

There was no leader in this musical production, just an unseen connection, a link that bound us and the cosmos together.

The night passed as overhead in the clear sky the full moon shone down, surrounded in its magnificence by billions of bright twinkling stars.

At one point when I allowed my arm a few moments of rest I leaned my body backwards and stared skyward gazing in wonderment at the constellations and galaxies.

Then I did a double take.

I closed my eyes and then reopened them.

I averted my gaze, and then refocused.

Each time I saw the same thing. There was one star shining

brighter than the rest. The brilliance of it was outshining those around it and the image I was seeing was something that I had never seen before,

It was rhythmically expanding and contracting.

It was not my imagination; this star, without any doubt, was pulsating. What was even more intriguing was that it was changing color and as it continued to pulse it became quite red.

I moved my head and looked towards the ground, I then resumed my gaze, and it was still there.

Siberian shamans claim an affiliation with the constellation of the Great Bear. In that moment I bitterly regretted my lack of knowledge of astronomy.

Was this phenomenon part of that group of stars?

Was it a spaceship?

Was it a communication from a non-earthly source?

It had been going on too long for it to be my imagination.

I continued to watch, totally transfixed, then slowly the pulsating slowed and stopped and the brilliance faded until it resumed its place as just one of a million stars and I resumed my drumming.

The first streak of light appeared in the sky and the night departed. It got lighter but still we continued drumming. All tiredness had long ago vanished. These natural sources had replenished our weary bodies and the events I had witnessed in the sky had stimulated my dull brain.

Out of the darkness the shapes of the few trees on this mountaintop resumed their clarity, a new day had dawned, and the night once again was over.

With the coming of the dawn all the drumming gradually slowed until, with us all following the lead of Moon Heart, it finally stopped and the shamans put their drums to one side.

But the ceremony was still not over. The shamans now began to sing and after about ten minutes we were told it was our turn and together after some discussion we recalled several favorite tunes from our childhood and were rewarded with laughter and loud hand claps from our hosts.

It was a wonderful way to bring the event to a finale.

The shamans now got on to their knees and placed their foreheads to the ground and the rest of my companions followed their lead. Apart, that is, from Mike who remained tucked up in his sleeping bag where he had lain all night, but as he later told us, extremely happy to be there and to feel part of the ceremony.

I felt the stiffness in my body as I moved and slowly lowered its weight onto my knees. Gingerly I put out my hands and rested the palms on the sharp stone and placed my forehead on the ground in a gesture of thanks to this wondrous Universe we are blessed to be a part of.

My whole being was vibrating from the drum sounds of the past few hours and my thoughts were filled with the beauty of the sights from the night sky, but as my forehead came into contact with the earth a spark akin to an electric charge entered my body at that exact point, right in the center of my forehead. Whatever it was, it came directly from the sacred tree that was standing about 100 yards away. I saw it shoot across the plateau, like a streak of lightning; it came just under the surface of the ground… It ran from the root of this special tree, across the open area and entered my forehead where it exploded into a million lights.

There was nothing presupposed or pre-suggested about it; thoughts of an occurrence such as this had never entered my mind.

It just happened!

The power of the experience was one that until now has been held close to my heart and a secret that I have previously shared with no one.

Slowly, one by one, we all got to our feet and this never to be forgotten solstice ceremony evoked a deep response within each member of the group. For as the new day grew ever lighter, we each without any instruction moved away from the ceremonial spot and instinctively all found ourselves a private place where we were content to sit for a while in solitude.

In the meantime Heurell ensured that every trace of the fire had been extinguished before the call went out to climb back into the jeeps.

Gisela, who had remained on the floor of the jeep all night, claimed to be feeling a little better although her pallor declared otherwise.

Mike was still very weak and unable to even stand, so our driver moved our vehicle the few yards from where it was parked and with a lot of help managed to ease Mike's large frame from where he still lay in his sleeping bag, close to the telltale remnants of the fire, into our transport.

I heard Rollanda say, "It's not very far," as she referred to the site of our next base.

This could mean anything and there was no point in taking her remark further, for we had all moved onto shamanic time and were accepting that everything happens when it is supposed to.

There was no mention of breakfast, but we were carrying plenty of drinking water, which, along with a shared bag of dried fruit and Trail Mix, sufficed.

We set off again, moved from this plateau and now began to make our descent.

From our start in Kyzyl we had traveled a long way south before traversing the mountains. Now we seemed to be heading in a westerly direction that quickly became a lot more forested, and after an hour or so we arrived in a vast valley. This was so different from the plains we had crossed the previous day for here it was lush and green.

It is difficult to appreciate the size and vastness of Siberia. Although this was a huge valley, it was but one of these many connecting troughs of land that run for hundreds of miles, divided by the many mountains that comprise the range of the

Sayans.

We passed a huge herd of sheep who all lifted their heads to watch us go by. Now we were just lurching along, trusting in our driver and the shamans we were following, for the track had long ago completely disappeared.

Suddenly galloping towards us came three men on horseback, their robes flying and in this unique setting I half expected to see them with daggers clutched between their teeth. It was a moment straight off a cinema screen.

A conversation ensued with our drivers, a dramatic way to ask directions, but within a short time we had sighted what would be our base for the next two nights. Tucked up on the line where the forest met with the open grassland was a one-room wooden building and alongside it two yurts had been erected.

This was the summer base of some nomadic people who were to be our hosts and they had temporarily vacated one of the yurts for the use of these Western strangers.

Without delay we pulled out our bags and entered our designated yurt. Heavy mats covered the floor, the potbellied stove that stood in the center was throwing out heat, and two single iron bedsteads sat on either side. In spite of their protests we helped Gisela and Mike onto each of them, and the sleeping bags of the rest of us were unrolled and filled with an occupant in a matter of minutes.

Sleep in preference to food was the prior demand of our bodies, but as I lay down, I suddenly had the urge to move and I got up, picked up my sleeping bag, opened the door of the yurt and stepped outside. Here I walked about twenty feet away and then like a dog circling its patch, did exactly this before laying it down on the ground and getting back into it!!

Chapter 8

It had already been morning and bright sunshine by the time we had finally climbed into our sleeping bags and fallen asleep, but only a few short hours later Rollanda was waking us all up and reminding us that this was not a site of R and R. We were to get ready for yet another ceremony!

I swiped at a swarm of mosquitoes that enveloped me as I climbed out of my sleeping bag and stood up. I looked around, and to my surprise I saw that about fifty yards away Moon Heart stood waiting as Natasha rolled up two sleeping bags. Those two had also chosen to sleep on the ground in the open.

I stretched my back and gazed around at the beautiful valley we were in. It looked peaceful and unthreatened, but the forested mountains that surrounded it were tinder dry. The river flowing into the valley that we had needed to cross to reach this camp was at an all time low. The goats and sheep that provided a livelihood for these people depended on water from this source, as they did themselves, so rain was a lifeline for them and this need was becoming urgent.

Looking up at the sky, I saw there was not a cloud in sight, just a huge expanse of blue and a heat in the sun that erased all memories of the cold of the previous night. The noise of the mosquitoes that buzzed around my head belied their size and I debated whether to change my short-sleeved top for something that would protect me from too many of their bites.

Both Gisela and Mike were feeling a little better, and somehow found a reserve of strength which was aided by a small portion of gruel. The rest of us also enjoyed a bowl of this hot breakfast, which we ladled out of an iron pot that sat bubbling on the stove.

One of our lady hosts had brought this to the yurt and amazed us with her strength as she heaved it up onto the top of the little potbellied stove which she had also fed by packing more wood into its belly.

The pair of them both insisted on attending this ceremony, which thankfully was taking place only a few feet from our residence.

This time we saw it was not related to an ovaa, but would be rituals to honor the spirits of this valley and would again include an invocation to the gods requesting rain.

Taking our drums with us we walked to where Ai-Churek was giving instructions to Vanessa, here about fifty yards away from the yurt. And at the edge of the forest we gathered and along with the drivers and every man, woman and child from this small nomadic family, we stood silently to witness the proceedings.

Once more the shamans were wearing their full ceremonial robes, complete with headdresses.

We waited and watched.

First a rope was strung between three trees to form a triangle, and then I saw that every one of us, including the smallest child, would be taking part for we were each given three strips of rag.

The instructions were translated for us by Rollanda. We followed these and again faithfully copied the other shamans by first tying our pieces of rag to the rope triangle. Next came the familiar offerings of bread and milk to the spirits, before Moon Heart produced a large piece of hollowed-out wood, and on this she placed small pieces of food, shells, leaves, large and tiny stones, and all manner of natural objects, chanting continuously as she did so. We watched as the other shamans began to sing and dance in and out of the triangle of prayer flags, and then they started drumming adding yet another dimension to the chanting.

The drum sounds slowly increased in tempo and then without missing a beat these women started to whirl, their robes flowing and the metal attachments that adorned them began to tinkle like small bells, which added a fairylike dimension to the deep vibration of the drums.

We stood with our Tuvan family hosts and watched this magical scene.

The message was then passed that we could participate and we enthusiastically entered this weaving circle, drawn in by the powerful energy, and added the sound of our drums to that of the shamans.

We drummed and drummed. My arms reached a point of pain where I felt I would just have to stop, but somehow I passed through it and continued without a pause moving into a trance-like state.

Who knows how long it continued, but I feel it was at least a couple of hours until finally the unheard signal to slow and cease finally arrived and spread through us all in a matter of seconds, until only the sound of Ai-Churek's drum continued. The rest of us sank to our knees, gently put our drums down and rested our foreheads on the pine needle-covered ground.

After a few moments the final drumbeat was played and all was quiet and still.

As I slowly moved back into normal awareness out of the trance-like state I felt something small tap down and hit my head. Then I felt it on my arms. Slowly I raised my head a little and opened my eyes; then I sat back on my heels and glanced up at the sky for confirmation.

What I had felt and seen were drops of rain!

The sky which at the start of the ceremony had been a huge expanse of clear cloudless blue was now filled with clouds, dark rain-filled clouds!

Drops of rain were falling from these clouds and pattering down, the volume increasing by the minute.

After a four-month drought this was the first signal that it was over.

With great hoots of laughter we made a rapid move for the

protection of the yurt. The sequence of events, with the synchronicity of the rain commencing the moment it had, were mind-boggling, and as we sat in the dry and poured milky tea from the jug sitting on the potbellied stove this subject filled the conversation.

We wrapped our hands around the mugs and looked out though the open door at a vista vastly changed from what it had been when we arrived here just a short time ago.

This was no gentle shower; the rain increased and soon it was tipping from the skies, a real deluge.

Our hosts scurried across from their base and brought a big pot of stew and bread for us. The weather was keeping us confined to quarters for a while but the enforced rest gave Gisela and Mike a chance to recover, and although they were both far from being 100% well they were certainly now on the road to recovery.

We wondered why out of all of us who were eating and drinking the same food, enduring the same living conditions, just two should be so very ill.

It was impossible to prove but the extended time that these two had put into the healings at Berdag was the only way their journey had differed from the rest of us and it seemed to indicate that it had been a drain on their own natural energies and immune systems. In view of the fact that they had both become so ill at the same time and so soon after leaving this village, this seemed the likely reason.

We lay in our sleeping bags napping and chatting while the heavy rain continued nonstop. Three hours later it was still falling and there was no sign of it abating.

It was at this point that Llyn became a little concerned. The journey here had been treacherous enough. She was responsible for the safety of six people and the rain was surely washing away at the tracks we had followed over the mountains. We had crossed several rivers that were reduced to a mere trickle, but the steep banks showed that a large volume of water had frequently passed its way.

"I am starting to get worried at this continuing rain. It is showing no signs of abating," she said and pulling on her waterproofs she headed out into the downpour towards the log hut in search of Rollanda and Moon Heart.

She was seeking reassurance that we would not become trapped in this valley, which to our eyes seemed a high possibility. She returned shortly offering us a choice.

"Moon Heart says there will be no problem and that we will leave tomorrow afternoon as planned.

However, if you would be happier to go now and not take any further risks that is what we can do.

Let's take a vote on it."

It was a difficult decision.

But we voted to stay.

Our belief in Moon Heart was resolute.

This woman seemed to be in partnership with the elements and bestowed with a power that emanated from a source beyond our comprehension. At that moment I would not have been surprised if she had waved a wand and turned our ancient jeeps into motorboats!

If she said there was no problem, I believed her.

Another three hours passed, the rain continued to fall unceasingly from a black sky with still no sign of it abating.

The shamans had brought across to us a bundle of material and with their instruction we had passed the time by ripping it into thin ribbon shreds and then carefully plaiting it to prepare a load of votive ribbons. Such a beautiful way to recycle and there was pleasure in doing this work.

There was no wind and still the rain continued its relentless downward fall and the huge sky above us remained dark with no sign of change.

My sympathies were with Llyn for I could see she was

decidedly nervous and fearful that we had made the wrong decision in voting to remain in this valley of Kala Hol.

Suddenly the small doorway of our yurt was filled by the figure of Heurell. He peered in, but remained outside with the water dripping off him and signaled to us to put on whatever wet weather gear we had and to follow him; his little English repeated the word "ceremony". There were groans from the sleeping bags; the grey weather and the lack of sleep had caught up on us and there was a distinct lack of enthusiasm.

But a little inner voice whispered to me, "You will regret not moving at this moment when you get back to England!"

Instantly I was up and the first one out.

This shaman was striding away across the now boggy grassland and I ran after him, pulling on my clothes as I did so.

He stopped and held up his hand. I stood beside him; the rest of the group were emerging from the yurt one by one and hurrying to catch up.

We stood in a huddle, the torrential rain instantly soaking us, dripping off the end of our noses and finding its way down the backs of our necks.

Some fifty yards away was the lone figure of Ai-Churek. She was again in her full shamanic regalia and stood with both arms held up to the dark sky. In one hand she held the large silver embossed conch shell.

Slowly she lowered her arms and putting the shell to her mouth, she blew into it. The long mournful sound grew ever louder and spread ever outwards. She turned and with a studied deliberation repeated this action four times, as she blew this sound into each of the cardinal points.

The sonorous echo traveled across the valley. It was absorbed into the wooded hills behind us and onto the barren mountains opposite.

The sound sent shivers through me and there was a sense of connection, as if I was traveling on the sound, moving through the air with the vibration and touching these mountains.

Then as I peered into the gloom, studying the mountains opposite, I saw a ribbon of light. It was not a ray of light coming downwards nor was it light from a thinning of the higher clouds. What I was seeing was a horizontal band of white and it was rising from behind these mountains.

At first it was visible only on the skyline in the lowest dips of this range. Then as it rose upwards, so it grew in length and was visible in the higher dips of these mountains. Soon it was above the tops of the smallest peaks.

A straight line of light and beneath it was a very pale blue sky, but totally cloud free. As this line moved upwards and above the top of the tallest piece of land, it felt as if someone was rolling the sky backwards.

There was a straight-ruled line between the black clouds still emptying heavy rain continuously over us and this band of white light heading our way. I likened it to being inside a sardine tin with the top being peeled back as it is opened.

Our jaws dropped, and with open mouths we stood in total amazement as we continued to watch this phenomenon.

We were oblivious to the soaking we were receiving, rooted to the spot as we watched the black portion of the sky slowly change and the blue portion increase its share of the heavens.

Still in a straight line, the dark fraction of the sky was diminishing, seemingly being pushed out of the way, and as it passed over our heads the rain immediately stopped, the sun was revealed and shone down on us from a cloudless sky.

One moment the water was tipping down on us – the next it had stopped!

I looked over my shoulder and I could still see it hitting the ground some distance behind us, but this too rapidly ceased, and within minutes the whole of the sky was devoid of clouds and a perfect clear blue in color.

Ai-Churek seemed satisfied and without further ado and a

single word she marched back to the log cabin.

We returned to the yurt, shook off our wet clothes and grabbed towels to dry ourselves. We were totally lost for words.

Searching for an understanding is pointless; to be witness to such powerful events is a blessing and is best just gratefully accepted.

We were all suffering from both mental and physical fatigue, but within a short time we were told to put on our warmest clothes, gather our drums and prepare for another ceremony!

In spite of the miraculous things we were seeing, all we wanted to do was lie down and sleep.

But how could we afford to miss anything?

What regrets we would suffer if when we returned to our conventional homes we should admit that we had by choice missed an opportunity to witness what these amazing Tuvan shamans could achieve?

With a supreme effort we got to our feet, put on our still wet clothes and made our way to the meeting point. A small open-backed lorry stood there along with the shamans who had traveled with us, plus every member of the nomadic family who were our hosts making up about a dozen assorted Tuvans milling around.

They were all talking and laughing. Their joy at the final arrival of rain was akin to hitting the Las Vegas Jackpot!

Then by a variety of means every one of us clambered aboard the lorry and proceeded on a journey that was equivalent to a roller coaster. A few white knuckles and a lot of prayer accompanied us on this trip as we headed in the direction of the far mountains behind which the band of light had arisen.

The lorry tipped and rolled precariously from side to side as we made our way over hillocks and across bog, and the shrieks were ones of fear, then gasps of relief.

The driver persevered until the vehicle sank to its axle and then we clambered down and continued on foot.

The sun was by now low in the sky and I had no idea what time it was but it was decidedly chilly and the temperature continued to drop. Added difficulty came as we were walking through wetlands. At first we tried leaping across the stretches of bog onto the solid looking hummocks, but these gave way like soggy cushions and our feet sank into the bog and the ice cold water, which at times came up to our knees. We continued this walk for thirty minutes and it was a relief to discover the small pudding-shaped hill now in front of us was our destination.

We huffed and puffed our way up the steep side to the top continually slipping in our soaking wet shoes.

At the top stood a single post held upright by strong rope stays. This marked the focus of our forthcoming ceremony and one by one we were passed a handful of the plaited rags and ribbons that we had prepared earlier.

These we attached to the rope stays. Once this was complete, chunks of bread were shared among us. We were now familiar with this ritual and, following the shamans' lead, broke it into small pieces, throwing it with gusto into the four directions shouting, "Take it! Take it!" to the spirits.

I stood and surveyed the land, looking out at the distance we had crossed to reach this point. A long way across the valley stood the tree-lined hills that protected our campsite. To my left across the valley I could see the route of the river from where it entered this area and ran down almost encircling this hill on which we stood. Then I turned my head and saw that it continued its journey further to where this plain spread out onto a large lake. It was late evening now and the water formed a large blot on the landscape justifying its name of Kala Hol, which translates as the Black Lake.

The sky, after the miraculous transformation as the rain ceased, continued to remain clear and cloudless and still a soft blue color.

We formed a large circle and stood in silence as we watched

Moon Heart perform a solo ritual. First she knelt in turn to the four directions, her lips moving as she uttered incantations, and then she got to her feet, looked up at the sky and began her drumming.

Within a few minutes a wind had blown up into this calm evening. It had suddenly appeared as if in response to her call. Her fellow shamans at this point joined in the drumming; and now with this added sound, the wind appeared to answer, for it rapidly increased its power and became quite strong.

I gazed around me looking out at the land and the river, the trees and the mountains, and then I tipped my head up to the vastness of this clear sky.

Almost as soon as I looked upwards I observed a single, small cloud appear over the far mountain. It came from the same point were the first white light had arisen only a few hours earlier.

There was just the one cloud, very large and bright red. It flew with the wind and like a great galleon sailed up from behind the mountain and headed towards us. Its outline was changing and it was moving rapidly in the now strong wind. It was quite high and my attention was fixed on it.

I saw the shape evolve into the form of a dragon!

Now it was a large image that replicated the ones of these creatures that are found in a child's picture book. It had the head, the ears, the long tail and the body which was supported by four short legs. It also had wings!

This cloud had a 'mackerel' effect that for all the world gave it the appearance of scales. It is difficult to estimate how long this cloud remained in the sky, but certainly for ten minutes or more.

All I know is that it flew right over us maintaining its brilliant red color until finally breaking up and petering out way over the tree-covered mountains behind our campsite.

All I can report is that it was the only cloud and the only sight in this otherwise unblemished sky.

The ceremony at this point came to a close and the light

started to fade. Rollanda called out to us. "We must hurry. Be quick now, hurry back to the lorry."

Across the swampland the lorry had extricated itself and was waiting to carry us back to the yurts.

As we half ran, half slid down the hill one of the older Tuvan ladies grabbed my hand. At first I thought she was looking for support, but then I realized she was offering me her assistance. She only came up to my shoulder and had an ancient lined face but her strength was unbelievable.

Tightly holding hands we jumped and ran and laughed as we flew across the hillocks. There was an overpowering sense of togetherness, and like two children running a three-legged race we moved as one.

Every one of us clambered back onto the lorry, which in spite of several times lurching at a dangerous angle somehow managed to stay upright and returned us safely to our base just as the last vestige of the light of day disappeared.

We were cold, wet and very tired but as we entered our yurt we found there was a hot stew bubbling away on top of the stove. One of these caring Tuvan women had obviously remained behind and missed the ceremony in order to prepare food and with every mouthful we blessed her.

At frequent intervals during the trip rational thoughts and questions kept peppering my mind, for our culture has a set pattern of how grandmothers are supposed to behave, and what I was doing here was way out of bounds.

The "What are you doing here?" continually arose. But even when I was stumbling around outside in the middle of the night in the cold and dark to answer a call of nature I would instantly dismiss them.

I had no answer. All I knew was that I was doing what I was destined to do. I was following my heart and in spite of all the difficulties it just felt right.

As we tucked down into our sleeping bags that night I heard

the voice of one of my companions come out of the darkness.

"Llyn, did you see that red cloud?"

And the response was,

"Yes. I think we all did. The dragon is an important part of the Tuvan culture and mythology. Just read your own message into it."

I fell asleep satisfied with the knowledge that if I had been hallucinating, so was everyone else!

At this time of the year, in this hemisphere the light vanishes for only a few hours. Like the birds I welcomed this darkness to close my eyes and rest, but it was not for long.

At first light I was awake and gingerly stepping over the prostrate and still sleeping figures of my companions. I quietly pushed open the door and went outside.

There was still a sharpness to the air and although the light was starting to spread across the valley the sun was still hidden behind the mountain.

I walked a short way and then sat leaving all signs of habitations behind me. Now I appeared to be alone in this vast valley with just my thoughts as companions.

My watch had been abandoned to a pocket inside my traveling bag. There was a release, an added sense of freedom in removing its need.

Time in this place had its own momentum.

How was it possible that I had arrived in this valley and only spent just the past twenty-four hours here? This fact seemed nonsensical for it felt as if I had been here for a long, long time.

I sat for a while before finally getting to my feet, and wandered a short way into the woodland looking at the variety of plants and wild flowers, but also being very careful to keep my eye on an exit. My 'homing instinct' is sharp but I had more sense than to test it in this wilderness.

As I made my way back to the yurt I saw signs of activity, and Galena was standing by the trees with their triangle of hanging rag offerings where only yesterday morning we had called on the rain spirits. She had been present throughout our journey generally helping out and assisting in the translation, and as we talked I realized this was her first exposure to shamanism and she was as awed by her countrymen as we were.

At every site starting in Kyzyl, where a ceremonial fire had been lit, she had gathered some of the ash and been keeping it safely in a glass jar. This she planned on sharing between us when our journey was over. It would be more than a memento, for there was a sense that this was sacred ash.

Diane had also made sure that throughout our journey and at every ritual the ball of string, that held the story and desires of each of us, had been placed in a position of prominence.

I arrived back at the yurt to find the large pot of breakfast gruel bubbling on the stovetop and helped myself to a bowlful, took it outside and sat on a log in the now warm sunshine knowing that the milk for it had come fresh from the goats just a short while ago.

Our time here had been brief, but once again it was time to move on and soon our sleeping bags were rolled up, bags packed and loaded back into one of the jeeps and after many thanks and goodbyes to our host family we all climbed aboard.

Mike and Gisela had by now fully recovered, but before we left this valley haven there was to be one more ceremony and as we drove around the far end of the Kala Hol Lake we suddenly came to a halt and followed instruction to all disembark.

Our 'Why and What' questions regarding the ceremonies had mostly gone unanswered. Sometimes Ai-Churek just turned on her heel, ignored the question and strode away; the only response we had from her was simply, "Watch me and do what I do". This recommendation I had unwittingly followed even to sleeping for those first few hours on the ground outside of the yurt when we first arrived at Kala Hol.

Thankfully that was only for a few hours, for the torment from the mosquitoes proved a severe test. But when, seeking a little sympathy, I moaned about this to Natasha, she shrugged her shoulders and said, "They won't kill you!"

Maybe there was no set pattern to any of the rituals that had been performed; we all had to discover our own personal route to communicate with the spirits. Constantly I reminded myself to be grateful to be having this amazing opportunity.

The ritual that was performed by her here was very different from all of the others. This time there was no ovaa, no fire, no drums and no votive ribbons.

At first we stood and watched along with Heurell and the other Tuvan shaman women as Ai-Churek alone donned her glorious feathered headdress, leaving the magnificent cape on the bank. And wearing a bright blue tunic over her trousers she waded out into the water until she was waist deep, the bright blue material floating out around her in sharp contrast to the darkness of the water.

The color of the lake had given it its name for I had never seen water this color and it was actually black. In the shallows you could not see below the surface and even where it lapped the shore it was still almost impenetrable.

Rollanda unable to relinquish her role of schoolteacher took control.

"Take your shoes off and line up!" she barked at us. "Facing the lake, in a row at the edge."

We took up our positions as she demanded.

The next order was to walk, keeping a straight line, into the water. It was impossible to see where each footstep would take us and there was a certain reluctance among some of the group to follow this simple instruction, so the line had a decided bend in it.

Surprisingly the temperature of the water was not the ice cold I had envisaged, but almost body temperature. However, it was difficult to walk for the bed of the lake was a combination of very soft mud, interspersed with slippery flint-like stones.

It was hazardous trying to maintain a balance but slowly we managed to form a line and moved until the level of the water reached just about the top of the legs of the shortest person. There we reached an impasse with this member refusing to take another step.

Rollanda, insistent at first on a straight line, now gracefully accepted this was as deep as we were going to go and avoiding a conflict deemed that this distance was acceptable.

Natasha then waded out to us, moved in front of us and stood at one end of the line facing us and holding aloft a large piece of wood. It was about three feet long and a foot wide and seemed to be a slice from a large log. On its flat surface lay an assortment of offerings and I noticed nuts, berries, stones, shells and small pieces of bread and cheese.

Rollanda's voice from her position on the bank carried out across the lake as she gave us instructions.

"Each of you in turn will take this altar, hold it carefully and raise it above your head. Silently you will give thanks to the spirits for the rain that has fallen, and honor the mountains and this sacred lake. Take your time, and then carefully pass it on to the person next to you."

She made us all nervous by adding, "Make sure you don't drop it!"

Natasha passed along in front of us and one by one, with her eyes fixed on each recipient, she presented the altar as she followed its progress. We each of us in turn and with considerable trepidation accepted the altar adorned with the offerings for the unseen energies, raised it high above our heads in an act of reverence, and having successfully accomplished the act, it was with great relief that we passed it back to her before it became the turn of our neighbor.

It was quite heavy and a sigh of relief was heaved by every single one of us when it reached the end of the line and was passed safely back into the capable hands of Natasha and our task was accomplished.

This slim assistant to the number one shaman then carefully waded out the considerable yards deeper into the lake to where Moon Heart had been standing observing the proceedings, and lowering her head in respect she passed it safely into her hands.

Now with her arms extended upwards, holding it high above her head, this shaman then turned in a full circle and dedicated the offerings to the four directions before lowering the votive and placing it on the water, where she gave it a gentle push and sent it heading out towards the center of the lake.

The drama we had witnessed during our stay in this beautiful valley was finalized with a ceremony of gentleness and reverence; a fitting conclusion to our stay.

Stumbling over the sharp stones, we quickly got out of the water as fast as we could, dried ourselves off and climbed back into the jeeps. We then continued making our way out of the valley as best we could which proved to be quite traumatic for it was not easy to find a place to cross the now swollen river.

Our driver finally found a spot he seemed happy with and having first made a few halfhearted attempts, committed himself and reached the point of no return, but as we moved off the bank into the water we tipped almost at right angles and we all held our breath.

It is preferable not to have too many moments like this, but at the same time it reinforces my belief that our time of departure from this life is already set and it will happen when it does.

I took my last look back at the valley and was overwhelmed with sadness. The ceremonies and the power of the place had unearthed deep feelings within me. My belief in reincarnation was strengthened by the fact that my heart hurt and I felt tears filling my eyes; the emotion belied the fact that I had spent only a few short hours in this glorious valley.

The hope that one day I could return was dampened by the

acceptance that it would be impossible to replicate the experiences of the last two days, but I knew nothing could erase the memory.

It was a long journey back to Berdag, one that was interspersed with periods of walking as a series of mechanical problems arose on one or another of the vehicles. When this happened the three-vehicle convoy came to a halt and all of the drivers combined peered into the engine or underneath it and made a group decision on the necessary repair.

Rather than just sit around most of us preferred to carry on walking. There was only the one track and the sky was clear and the weather was warm. We took our time and the others invariably caught us up.

It was during the first of one of these periods when we reached the spot where we had held the Summer Solstice ceremony. We had been trekking on this rough ground for a while and Sam and I who had been walking side by side decided to take a break.

Once again I saluted the Sacred Tree and performed the ritual of moving three times around its base on my knees, before joining Sam where she sat in the shade of a tree and we both delighted in resting our weary joints.

This was such a magical spot, it simply oozed 'atmosphere' and for a few moments we sat in total silence. I could feel a myriad of invisible spirits and I looked at the ground where that bolt of light had traveled across, almost expecting to see some visible sign of its journey on this rough surface

The memory of that all-night drumming was still so fresh and my friend then confided in me and shared one of her personal experiences of that unforgettable night.

I listened as she said, "You remember the moment when Ai-Churek asked the other shamans to rest and for just our group to drum?

What happened was an incredible moment for me.

This is the first time I have owned a drum. I have always wanted one, but somehow never got around to buying one.

I guess because Heurell says the drum chooses you and mine was waiting here for me in this country.

Well just as we were starting to play, Ai-Churek leaned across and passed me her beater to play with. I don't know why. But I put mine down and took hers.

It was quite extraordinary, for while I was using it, it seemed to have a life of its own. I promise you, the beater was doing the drumming. I felt like its shadow just following it. It was incredible and is such a difficult sensation to describe or try to explain."

I could feel the emotion filling her and she stopped briefly before continuing.

"It's impossible to prove. But I just know it happened. The feeling was so amazing. It was like some sort of magic."

I tipped my head, glancing sideways at her. "You are aware of the shape of the beater our respected shaman uses, aren't you?" I said, expecting an affirmative response. Instead she looked at me blankly.

"Oh, Sam!" I laughed. "The wood is carved in the shape of an arrow! Your retrieval tool! That special gift you were given by the spirits. Remember?"

She sat there and her jaw dropped open, she could not speak!

Then we both burst into laughter.

It was yet another magical moment.

Chapter 9

Sam and I got back onto our feet, stretched ourselves and then continued our walk, the vehicles eventually caught up with us and our long and tiring journey continued.

Our first planned stop was at the village of U-Shina where we were greeted by many smiling faces. Here the visible signs of the land having been recently hit by heavy rainfall were apparent and the reason for these signs of joy.

The residents poured out of their houses to see us all, but our stay was brief and we were quickly on our way again.

Then as we finally drove back into Berdag we noticed the ditches were running water and the clouds of dust that had previously arisen from the wheels of our convoy were now no more.

Everywhere that we had performed a ceremony focusing on the request for rain had over the past few days received an abundance of this element.

It was magical and gratifying, and also very humbling.

From Berdag we no longer had need of the four-wheel drive transport and we returned to the familiarity of our ancient coach and as many people as possible climbed in.

Leaving the village I observed its residents waving goodbye until we were almost out of sight, then we turned a corner and headed back for suburbia and the town of Kyzyl.

I sat on the backward facing seat at the front of the bus, and as we set off I glanced around at my companions observing how the effects of this tough journey with the additional lack of sleep showed clearly on their faces.

In spite of the satisfaction of achieving our purpose there was a slight disconsolate air as we accepted that this adventure was moving towards its end.

I watched as the sight of the powerful Red Mountains began to recede ever further and felt a boulder of distress rise up from the depths of my guts. In the momentary second that I became aware of this emotion, and before there was any visible sign, the two shamans sitting on the seat opposite both simultaneously reached out their hands to me.

Nina and Vera, both powerful shamans, in tune with the energies all around them, live constantly in the present. They picked up my pain at the same instant that I became aware of it and were immediately there with comfort.

Their lives are spent with a richness we can only dream about. We compare lives and presume they are suffering materially, but their wealth comes from a source that we in the West only briefly glimpse.

It was the early hours of the morning after first unloading the shamans and their belongings at the Tos Deer Clinic before we finally reached our hotel. And once back in the bedroom it felt very claustrophobic to be confined within four walls and I had to leave the door leading onto the small balcony wide open to ease this feeling.

We were back up and downstairs ready for breakfast by 8.30 am. There would be time enough to catch up on our sleep when we returned to our homelands.

There was to be a final meal and a celebration at the Tungar Clinic on the waterfront this coming evening. A time to say thank you and make our goodbyes to the shamans with whom we had spent this brief, but unforgettable journey, and with this in mind we planned our day.

We agreed we wanted to wear something special for this occasion, something traditional and essentially Tuvan, so the morning was designated for shopping in search of suitable apparel.

How spoilt we are in the West with the focus of our culture's economy based on consumerism. It did not occur to us that because our wallets had the necessary dollars to purchase what we required the articles we sought would not be available. There were quite a few shops with their doors open but inside they were the same, with mostly bare shelves and very little to buy. Audio tapes were on sale and most of the shops sold buttons. In fact if you wanted buttons, there was a great variety and you had a choice; it seemed a strange item to be plentiful.

As we made our way through the town we passed quite a few shoe shops, but very little else. Finally Galena stopped a passerby who suggested a place that required a taxi ride to get there.

We were determined to make the effort with our appearance for this final evening and piling into a couple of cars that would not have been allowed anywhere near a public area in our home countries, we set off.

The roads were in a desperate state of repair and full of potholes and at times the driver, without reducing his speed, put his hand down hard on the horn to warn pedestrians and simply took to the pavements in an effort to avoid them.

Somehow I had ended up sitting in the front, alongside him. I must have been the slowest getting into the car because it was obviously the seat to avoid as the windscreen in front of me had large deep cracks running across it and over every bump I closed my eyes half expecting it to fall in on top of me.

We finally found the store we were seeking and walked into one very large but almost bare room.

Instantly I spotted 'it'!

This item stood alone on a small chest at the end of this room.

It was there waiting for me, the rapport was instant, it was something special and I knew, without question that it belonged to me.

'It' was a headpiece, too grand to be called a hat and even more beautiful than a crown. This wonderful cone-shaped concoction was about two feet tall and stiffened with something unseen that gave it a fluted shape. It was covered in a glistening shimmering silver material that ran upwards and finished in a point. The edge of the turned-up brim also smoothly shaped itself, into a point on either side above the ears.

A laced piece of strung pearls hung in a triangular shape on either side of the brim giving the effect of large ornate earrings and two lengths of wider silver ribbon were attached, ready to tie under the chin of the wearer to secure it in position.

Pearls and diamante ran along the top side of the brim, and these also ran up the sharp edge of the fluting where they were tied at the top, and then a surplus length of about 6 inches of each of the five strands swung downwards.

It was magnificent!

Like a magnet pulling me, my feet took me directly across the bare wooden floor towards it, where with both hands I reverently lifted it and claimed it.

I knew it was mine. Taking it to where the lone shop assistant was standing alongside the till I placed it down, perched myself on a stool next to it and prepared to wait while my companions looked around to try and fulfill their needs.

A few silk and embroidered waistcoats and jackets were hanging from a string that was pinned across one wall and my friends made a beeline for these.

These items in our search for party wear were the sole reward of our morning's quest.

I sat and watched while they tried and considered and exchanged between themselves these few vestments, for there were exactly six of these articles for sale and I had no interest in acquiring one.

My purchase would probably seem to others to be quite ridiculous, but I knew it was right for me. There was absolutely no question. Some innate knowledge left me in no doubt that it was what I was meant to wear.

Finally the robes and waistcoats each found the right owners and we were all happy. We paid for them, jumped back into the waiting taxis and returned to the hotel, well satisfied with a successful morning's shopping.

A quick freshen up, a bite of lunch and we returned along the dusty streets for a final visit with Professor Kenin Lopsan.

On our earlier visit he had requested information regarding the birthdates of all of us. And now at this meeting he shared with us the information he had discovered by preparing a chart of our lives which was all based on the date, time and place of our entry into this world.

From this chart he disclosed events that had already influenced our past and gave each of us an indication of what the future held and what was destined to be our life mission.

From our birthdate he could detect the main strengths and weaknesses in our character and foresee personal major events that would color and influence our lives.

He confirmed for me my belief that I have more than a superficial link to this country, for he claimed there were indications in my chart of past lives spent in Tuva. And this he felt was confirmed by the fact that the sacred number in his country is number nine and with my birthday being on the ninth of the ninth, he placed great importance on this fact.

These sequential numbers have proved in the past to have great impact on my life and his mention of them reminded me of an event in 1999.

About a month before my birthday in this year my husband casually asked me, "Where would you like to go for your birthday this year?" He was probably thinking more on the lines of a special restaurant for dinner, but without a moment's hesitation, these words came out of my mouth.

I heard myself say, "Machu Picchu!"

I am still unsure as to who was most shocked, him or me.

I had no idea where they came from and we stood there looking at each other in total silence.

Finally he said, "Do you really?"

All I could manage was a weak, "Yes."

But arrangements were made and on the night of the 8th

September we stayed in the small hotel adjacent to the gates of this incredible place, then shortly before dawn on my birthday the 9.9. 1999, and leaving my husband sleeping soundly, I was up and out of the hotel and waiting surrounded by thick mists outside the gates of the Sacred and mystical complex known worldwide as Machu Picchu.

The guard unlocked the gate and that day I was the first one to walk through the entrance where I stepped into a strange stillness, all sounds were muffled and the visibility in the mist of this cloud forest was less than 50 yards.

I had no plan and just allowed my legs to take me. After a while I found myself ascending a long flight of stone steps until I reached a small plateau where I turned and sat down on the edge and surveyed what were but vague shapes in the mist. Nothing moved – no humans, no llamas and there was no sound.

Just total silence.

I closed my eyes and began to meditate.

I felt cocooned. It was as if I was inside an egg and it seemed as if the powerful energy of this place was the shell enclosing me.

It was the strangest feeling, one of absolute isolation but also a sense of being complete.

Then the egg/me started to grow; it expanded ever outwards. And I experienced a primordial connectedness with the All as a sense of being wrapped in a love beyond description enveloped me.

It was intense but probably lasted only a few short seconds before it faded and I opened my eyes.

The mist was a little thinner but otherwise nothing in front of me had changed; but I discovered in that brief moment a small brown dog had joined me and was now sitting by my side. His position was the same as mine, with his front legs firmly placed and upright, exposing his white chest that faced outwards down the mountainside, but his head was turned up and his eyes were looking directly up into mine.

His ears were not a matching pair, for although one stood upright the other turned over, giving him a slightly quizzical look. While not a puppy he was certainly a young dog and one with what I instantly sensed was a friendly demeanor.

We sat together for a few minutes with neither of us moving, but then the chill of the morning started to seep into my bones and I got up and decided to walk some more. Without any bidding the dog accompanied me, walking close to my heels, stopping when I stopped and continuing when I chose to.

The thick mist was by now starting to thin and lift and through the gloom the shape of the mountains was beginning to be revealed. In one area the sky was definitely lighting up and starting to glow.

It was apparent that the sun would soon break through and herald the dawn of a new day.

Quickly I scanned the area around me and spotted a position where I could observe the first glimpse of the sunrise.

It would be my birthday treat to fully participate in this most natural of ceremonies, this daily event which has occurred for eons.

I quickly moved up another flight of steps with the little dog leaping nimbly alongside.

As I reached a small plateau I was disappointed to find a couple of people already there, for I really felt the need to be alone, but it was too late to move elsewhere and I just hoped they would observe the sunrise in silence.

The two men stood with their cameras at the ready, one peering though the lens of one that was set up on a tripod, the other poised with his held close to his face. Both of them were focused on the task ahead and ready to capture the moment.

I scanned the area looking for somewhere to sit down and at this time another man and woman entered the plateau from the other side and they walked towards the center where there was a solitary large square stone.

This stone was about a three–four feet square cube, and although I would definitely have preferred solitude I suddenly felt myself drawn towards it and walked, positioning myself behind it facing out into the valley and the sky where the now imminent first ray of the sun was about to appear.

This looked like a perfect spot for there was a straight clear view opposite to where a dip in the mountains revealed the sky at its brightest; it was here that the first rays of the morning sun would come.

I stood up straight and focused on the point where I felt the first ray of sun would appear.

The little dog made no attempt to seek out the friendship of these other people, choosing instead to ignore them and he positioned himself at my feet.

The sky took on a pink, then a yellow glow as we awaited the sun. The light started to spread in the sky, even before the orb from which the light was emanating appeared between the mountains. Such was its power that the mist rapidly withdrew and the chill in the air vanished.

I sat quietly composed, wrapped in the peaceful stillness. The first brilliant rays appeared and I felt the light strike my forehead.

It was as if I had been struck by a bolt of lightning, such was my dramatic reaction. One moment I was relaxed and in quiet anticipation, the next I had flung my arms outstretched as wide as possible as an unseen but powerful force poured into the top of my head.

It all seemed to happen simultaneously, but before I could even think what was happening I threw myself on to my knees and placed my forehead on the ground as great almost electrical shudders passed through me.

Finally I prostrated myself, with arms out at right angles to my body as further waves of electric-like charges rippled through me. I lay there unmoving until slowly this force started to ebb away and I found myself gently crying.

These actions had been instantaneous and automatic. Somehow there had been a removal of all my physical control, all egotistical feelings and all inhibitions; everything had been totally swept away, leaving me an empty shell.

My outward projection of a reserved lady of middle years fell away as I succumbed wholly to a split between consciousness and body.

Some active and ancient force beyond human understanding had been triggered and I was in a state of shock. But I quickly returned to my normal level of understanding and as I lay there in the dirt an acute feeling of embarrassment swept through me.

With some haste I scrambled to my feet, fumbling for tissues to wipe my face and blow my nose. Keeping my head down and in a state of shock, I hurriedly looked for an exit to this plateau.

The little dog that had remained by my side now seemed to lead me out of this area and he guided me between two pillars before we started down a long flight of narrow stone steps. Then with him walking just one step in front of me we began to descend. We had gone about a quarter of the way down in this manner when I noticed two women with a man close behind them, in single file and coming up.

It requires lungs full of air to climb on these mountains at these altitudes; only children and the super fit can climb and talk at the same time. These people were not young and were reserving all of their energy for the physical effort this required; they moved slowly and quietly and in no way presented an aggressive image.

To my surprise the little dog stopped and let out a menacing growl.

Startled they looked up at him. He repeated the warning only this time it was louder. His hackles went up. They stopped and stood still. Then staring at them he curled back his upper lip and bared his teeth, all the while continuing with the deep-throated growl. They recoiled in horror. The image this dog projected transformed him. This sweet little dog had become an animal of ferocity, the hair on his back was erect, and standing up like porcupine bristles; and these people froze as the dog maintained his pose.

Then I head a man's voice call out and with great authority he said,

"Move over to your right and then stand perfectly still." Then he added,

"He's a guardian dog. Let him and the lady pass."

The ladies were transfixed in their fear. Slowly and cautiously they followed this order and the gentleman also responded to the instruction.

Once they had moved sufficiently, little dog seemed appeased, his hairy coat started to flatten, his lip dropped, but slightly stiff legged he walked past. He glanced over his back as if checking that I had safely passed them, and then assuming his earlier attitude bounced on down the steps, keeping at my pace.

This dog and I continued to wander around the site for a few hours. Several times people stopped to try and give him a pat, but he moved out of reach showing no further aggression, just total indifference, choosing to reject their advances. He remained with me, only leaving the proximity of my heels when I walked back into the hotel lobby. I came out about 30 minutes later with some scraps of food I had saved from breakfast but I never saw him again.

Later when I was back in Cusco and without sharing this story, I asked an elderly Peruvian guide if he knew anything about the stray dogs at Machu Picchu.

He looked at me thoughtfully and replied, "Aah! The temple guardians." Then he volunteered, "Occasionally one of these dogs will appear and attach itself to one it considers special. It will remain with them while they are in the Sacred Place."

Then he gave an enigmatic smile and walked away.

Before I left Peru I purchased a book at the airport called *The Awakening of the Puma*, which carries information on ancient initiation rites and a picture of a re-enactment on page 153 shocked me.

The photo showed a woman at Machu Picchu, standing in exactly the same place as I had serendipitously been standing at dawn on 9.9.99 with the first rays of the morning sun striking her forehead.

The caption underneath read:

"The priestess receives the sun's light on her forehead. The initiation directly given by Pachamama and Wiracocha had begun."

The two names the ancient inhabitants of these lands gave to our planet and the sun.

Leaving this memory behind I focused once more on the words of Mongush Kenin Lopsan as he continued to share with my companions the information he had gleaned from their respective birthdates.

This gentleman then extended our visit to him by showing us around a normally locked area set to one side of the building that housed the museum.

Here in an unroofed area, enclosed by just a simple wooden fence, stood a great many mostly unseen treasures, ancient stone statues that had been unearthed over the years. They stood here like refugees patiently waiting for the funding to house them. These relics far removed from their original sites still held their energy; each had a distinct presence.

Rollanda did a wonderful job of translating. So much of this man's knowledge has been passed down verbally and he has made it his life's mission to seek out the few remaining elders to glean and record this wisdom.

The sun burned directly overhead. The professor is not a well man and in the hot sunshine he continually mopped his brow. He was trying to balance his duties as a host and share his passion for these artifacts with his personal well-being. As we walked through the long uncut grass, clouds of mosquitoes flew up adding to our mutual discomfort and we were tormented by the irritating buzz and unceasing bites from the swarms of insects.

It was decidedly uncomfortable for everyone and after posing for a group photo with us, and with a great reluctance, he brought our visit to a close and we bade our farewells and returned back to the hotel.

There was never a free moment. Now there was time only to pack, ready for a very early departure the next morning, to freshen up and to dress in our finery ready for the evening events.

Throughout our travels, except when the rain was torrential, I had been wearing a pair of silver shoes. These I put on once again and at the bottom of my bag I retrieved a rolled up white dress that I had been guided to pack, an unlikely item but one the voice in my head insisted I pack!

I draped one of the Khata scarves around myself and was happy with the effect.

A short while later we all met up in the hotel lobby and then set out on the short walk to the Tungar Clinic.

We attracted many stares as we made our way there, the tunics and waistcoats were stunning, each in a different color and the beadwork shone and sparkled as the light from the low evening sun bounced off it.

Sitting firmly on my head was The Hat. It fitted as if it had been tailor-made and there was a sense of wearing something so much more than merely a piece of head wear.

A strange energy was being transmitted from it giving me a feeling that I had certainly never experienced before. I kept telling myself that I was 'imagining' something, but deep in my heart I was aware of a ripple of something that I sensed was non-ordinary.

What I was sensing was impossible to describe, so I said

nothing for I had neither the words nor a reason to explain or share it.

My companions were all carrying their drums; I carried only my beater/rattle. I had left my drum in the room, but not forgotten for when I had gone to pick it up the guiding voice in my head very clearly said, "Leave it!" and I had adhered to this instruction.

There felt something almost bridal about my headwear, but Rollanda had not offered any explanation about the source of this design or the normal ceremonial occasion on which it would be worn. I in turn had not been drawn to ask. It was immaterial. At this point I was so in touch with my feelings I was swept along with a conviction that all was exactly as it should be and part of the great Universal Plan.

A large crowd was milling around the space between the two yurts as we reached the clinic. Word had got around that a ceremony with the foreigners would be taking place tonight; it seemed we would have a big audience. Some were there with the intention of participating, much like a church congregation. Others were merely curious and a few had collected as they do everywhere simply because they had noticed others standing around and had nothing better to do.

Leaving our shoes outside, we were ushered this time into the second yurt, the one standing on the far side. This had no furnishings only a floor covering, which Rollanda invited us to sit down on before she began to speak.

She explained that this yurt had not yet been used for the clinic community, as tradition holds that before it is put into action important and honored guests must first be greeted and offered hospitality under its roof.

We had been chosen for that role and were delighted that after a week of constant scrutiny, as we traveled with these powerful shamans, this was the proof that we had gained their approval and this we considered an award.

I harbored a thought that the wearing of The Hat was providing an additional lesson for me as its height made it necessary for me to drop to my knees every time I passed through a doorway and thus evoked a nuance of humility.

We were served tea and little fruitcakes and cookie delicacies. Then Rollanda reminded us that there were a lot of people waiting to commence the ceremony.

We were totally unaware that they were waiting for us, but as we emerged from the yurt I saw what she meant. Work had finished for the day and even those who had ventured out for an evening stroll had been attracted by the throng and stopped.

While we had been enjoying our tea many more numbers had been added to the assembly and the crowd seemed to have doubled.

Earlier Llyn had asked Rollanda to provide an opportunity during this time for us to present Moon Heart with a gift.

This was an item Llyn had had the foresight to bring with her, but she wished to present it on behalf of us all. It was a small brass bell, not of great monetary value, but priceless because of its association. It had originated in a temple in Tibet, been given to her by a friend who had come to America via India and this unique item had been used to call the spirits to join and bless many ceremonies in these different lands.

Now it was to be passed into the safe hands of this powerful Tuvan shaman.

Our interpreter was also aware of how the evening's proceedings had been planned by our hosts. Rollanda took charge of this moment and relishing her role she acted like the head mistress at a school assembly and lined us all up.

Moon Heart flanked by the other shamans stood opposite us. But before any exchange of gifts could take place this woman broke ranks and launched into one of her commanding oratories.

There was a large crowd and she was not going to miss this opportunity of exhorting them to resume a personal responsibility. She was forthright in encouraging them to discover their inner strength and recognize their individual power; with our interpreter working rapidly we appreciated what a masterful speech it was and witnessed its visible impact.

We were each then presented with another Khata scarf. I have always been open to other religions and beliefs feeling they are simply different ways up the same mountain and these shamans seemed to have no difficulty in incorporating and honoring aspects of other dogmas into their own tradition.

This was the third one we had received and I wondered if this time they would remain in my keeping or would I once again be used as a messenger as I had two years ago when one of these had been placed around my neck directly from the hands of his Holiness the Dalai Lama.

Now Llyn had her opportunity to present the gift to Ai-Churek and the little bell that had made its long journey found a new home.

Rollanda then for the final time translated the sequence of what would be our last joint ceremony with these incredible Tuvan shamans as she said:

"In accordance with tradition Michael as the only male among you has been given the honor of preparing and lighting the fire. The wood is chopped and ready and under the guidance of Heurell he will set and light this last bonfire. The rest of you with our shamans will witness this ritual by kneeling in a circle at the edge of it. Once the fire is burning, Michael will stand and start the drumming. Then one by one, as you feel ready, you too will stand and join in the drumming, then begin to slowly move around the flames. The Tuvan shamans will follow and step in and join you."

Michael and Gisela had by now fully recovered from their sickness and were thankfully back in good form. We took up our places and watched as Michael picked up the first sticks; then, with Heurell by his side closely supervising him, he reverently stacked them in the appropriate format. Three sticks at a time were set down before another layer was added, and ever mindful of the sacred number nine the fire was built.

Our male companion then picked up the box of matches and with due solemnity removed one, struck it and held the flame under the stack of wood. We held our breath as a spiral of smoke ascended, we then breathed a sigh of relief as it burst into flames. He knelt for a few more moments looking deeply into these flames, and then with great deliberation he picked up his drum and slowly got to his feet. He stood there resplendent in his green silk embroidered jacket, and then struck the first sound. His beater produced a deep boom as it bounced off the drum skin, and as I watched him I realized I was looking at a fully-fledged shaman. One by one everyone around the fire got to his or her feet, and as they did so the volume of the drumming increased.

I alone was still on my knees.

It felt as if there was a strong magnetic pull coming from the ground and holding me there. A voice in the corner of my brain was shouting at me saying, "Stand up! Stand up!" But my body refused this order.

Almost simultaneously a strong unseen presence started to form around me and I felt it drawing ever closer, tightening in on me.

My eyes closed and I felt myself slipping into a void. I could hear the drums beating but they seemed far off; the sound was coming from somewhere away in the distance.

I was slipping into a duality.

Within seconds I had the sensation of my awareness being moved out to the sidelines and as this other persona slipped into my mind it became dominant, took control of my body and left me as a mere spectator. Still on my knees I was aware of my body rocking backwards and forwards, then with eyes still closed I got to my feet and stretched my arms straight up into the air above my head, and holding this posture I turned and saluted the four directions.

Then my mouth opened and out of it came wolf-like calls which echoed around my body as I turned and started to continuously spin.

There was a surreal air to this 'possession' but I had already learned from past experiences that this split always runs its course and the 'I' part of my consciousness surrenders and waits in the background until the force inhabiting me has finished.

In due time I sank back to the ground and quite swiftly the energy detached and then distanced itself from me. The drumming continued and I remained back on my knees with my eyes closed. Once for a few brief moments I felt the presence return and I recall lifting my head, but I moved no further, and without rising to my feet simply tilted my head back and then heard these strange calls emitting from my throat.

Who or whatever it was then departed and shortly after that I felt myself returning to normality. This change in consciousness ran concurrent with the fading of the sound of the drums and as the last drumbeat sounded my eyes opened.

The ceremony was over and I got to my feet. There was a distinct change in the level of energy from when we had started. It was palpable and I felt disorientated.

Almost simultaneously the crowd around us suddenly surged forward and there was a moment of intense apprehension as we became engulfed in a sea of Tuvan men, women and children, but above it all I could hear Rollanda's voice shouting, "Don't be afraid! Please don't move! These people just want to touch you and shake your hands."

At first it was quite intimidating as they all flocked around us for it was so unexpected. We were relieved when it somehow fell into a natural order of a patient spiraling queue. It seemed every man, woman and child that had observed the ceremony wished to touch us, to shake us by the hand or to give us a big hug. It was an expression of their feelings, open and totally without reservation.

Rollanda later voiced the opinion that they felt by touching us some of the energy of the spirits that had been drawn into the circle by our actions would be transmitted to them.

Finally it thinned out and I noticed a young man who was standing slightly back from the crowd observing me closely. He looked to be in his early twenties, quite tall and thin. He had blond hair and very clear light blue eyes. His physical features defined him as Russian rather than Tuvan and as the last of the crowd finally petered out and moved away and we prepared to leave, he came forward towards me.

In excellent English he asked "May I speak with you please?"

I held out my hand and said, "Of course."

He began with a question that took me aback.

"What is the name of the entity that you channel? I feel he comes from far out in the Cosmos. I would like to know which Planet he comes from."

He was very serious. I stifled a giggle as his words immediately evoked a memory of a moment during our time at Kala Hol.

While we were confined to the yurt waiting for the torrential rain to ease I had need to leave the comfort of the yurt to answer a call of nature. Our baggage for this trip had, of necessity, to be minimal so my wet weather gear consisted of a hooded poncho made of a reflective silver material and I was wearing this and also my silver shoes.

As I returned to the yurt Llyn, Sam and Jennifer were peering out of the open doorway giggling like schoolgirls.

"We wondered what it was," they spluttered. "Even the cattle were staring! We though some one had landed from Outer Space!"

Fortunately, I bit my tongue and responded to the young man with due consideration.

However, there was not much I could tell him. I shared with him the fact that this was the first time this entity had used me as a tool and I was not familiar with it. However, I had perceived a feeling of gentleness so I shared this with him and also added that I felt it was in no way threatening and there was a sense of strength rather than power. Other than this there was little I could add.

He seemed satisfied with these few words and before saying goodbye added,

"I liked him very much."

On all of our previous visits to the clinic we had remained in the confines of the yurts. Now one last memento of our stay in Kyzyl remained for before we finally left the premises Heurell invited us into the main clinic building and extended to us the opportunity to view the room in which he treats patients.

What a sight greeted our eyes!

It was decorated with a multitude of objects. Hanging from the walls and laid on numerous small tables was a vast collection of shamanic regalia. There were feathers, drums, rattles, animal skulls, skins and furs. All of these aids for calling on the assistance of the elements and ancestors to join in the healing, to help guide the shamans through any trance states and for protection when entering battle with hostile forces.

There were jars of herbs and bottles of lotions and medicine bundles. Sprigs of sage and other plants used to smudge and cleanse. On one table I saw an animal shoulder blade bone, probably from a sheep, for this I knew was used and much favored by Siberian shamans in the act of divining.

Rocks of varying sizes often thought to be containers for spirits were sitting around.

Hanging in one corner in the pose of supervisor were the robes he donned to perform these duties as a shaman for the community.

The overall picture looked like the dressing room for a

pantomime, but I knew that it was all for real, sacred and precious.

The image was an abiding one that we carried with us, not just as the finale of our stay in Tuva, not just into our dreams that night; this was yet another memory to carry forever.

We moved outside and turned to leave. At that moment Heurell's wife hurried up to me, she bowed then held out her cupped hands, enclosed in which she had a gift for me.

She placed a small silk bag pulled tight with a drawstring. I graciously accepted it and gave her a hug before we both turned away to go in opposite directions.

On returning to the hotel I looked at this precious gift.

This lady had passed into my keeping her personal set of stones and seeds that she used for divination and I at that moment committed myself to being worthy of this gift.

Chapter 10

After a few short hours' sleep and a hurried breakfast we climbed onto the coach to set off on the long ride back to Abakan.

We had given our thanks and said our goodbyes to Rollanda before we departed. She had arrived at an early hour in the morning to wish us well as we returned to our own countries. We had turned and waved as we drove off, our hands continuing to flap until we rounded a corner and she was out of sight.

There was no doubting the effort she had put into trying to make our visit a success, and she was always aware of how important it was to her community that the impression we carried away with us was a favorable one.

The job she had performed was a balancing act. Her English was almost perfect although she had never traveled out of Russia, and I am sure had no idea how unaccustomed we all were to the lack of basic facilities and the arduous physical difficulties we had encountered.

So intense had been our relationship with the shamans that there was a sense of amputation, a definite pain of loss, and as the miles went past we each sat engrossed in our personal memories and thoughts.

There was a very subdued atmosphere and we all slept inter-mittently as our vehicle covered the many miles back to Abakan. We alighted from the coach only to pay homage to the spirits as we crossed a mountain pass or when we spotted an ovaa, this mark of a sacred place, when we again left to briefly offer up prayers.

Galena remained with us on the drive as she was our link between the two languages, guiding us through the border crossing and the purchase of edible provisions which we ate on the way straight to the airport. She accompanied the seven of us until she had completed her responsibility, got us checked onto our flights and watched us move through to a very basic departure area to await the flight back up to Moscow.

It must have been with a great sigh of relief that she made her way back to the familiarity and comforts of her own home, where she could tuck away the memories of her journey with tales to be brought out for her grandchildren some time way in the future.

The extent of our experience of the vagaries of traveling in this part of the world had not yet ceased. For when we walked out some distance onto the edge of the runways to board our plane we discovered that the rules of safety and security that protect but restrain our freedom in our home countries were nonexistent.

Maybe having a private pilot's license makes me more observant of aircraft and their requirements, but I noticed that the concrete of the runway was both pitted and broken, and our transport was an aged rear-loading prop plane.

As we joined the queue to ascend the staircase and board I was astonished to see a small pack of dogs run up to us in search of scraps of food, then after retrieving a stale sandwich thrown by someone we watched as they engaged in a play/fight around the wheels of the aircraft.

A few minutes later I saw two men emerge at the top of the steps and start to squeeze themselves down past the ascending passengers. They were both wearing uniforms, and by these and their caps I identified them as the pilot and co-pilot. Once at the bottom of the steps they walked a few feet to one side, where, to my horror, I witnessed them both standing close to the airplane's full tanks of avgas and lighting up cigarettes!

Our lives were in the lap of the gods, but they must have been smiling on us for finally after twenty-four hours of almost nonstop traveling we fell into our beds in a hotel alongside the famous Red Square in Russia's capital city.

Our sleep and time to rest was brief for we had just a few

hours to spend in this most splendid of cities, to view the stunning architecture and the overwhelming beauty of St Peter's.

Here it was a world away from the sights of the past ten days, and I found it almost impossible to merge back into the consumerism and commercial activity that surrounds tourists on this hill.

There was a dreamlike quality to the morning as I wandered around and purchased a few souvenirs. We were all having great difficulty in orienting ourselves and there was a feeling we were like aliens newly arrived on this planet.

Before the car with an English-speaking escort arrived to take us back to Moscow's international airport we held one last ceremony.

The seven of us gathered in one of the dull, bleak bedrooms where Llyn with a few beautiful and well-chosen words stirred the memories and images of our journey and presented each of us with a little bag containing ash from the fires that had burnt during the rituals and ceremonies we had all shared. It was wood from the trees of Siberia that had been shape shifted by the flames into this ash, thus becoming a tangible symbol of the prayers that had been offered to the gods and spirits.

Our intrepid leader then produced the length of string that has been carried throughout our travels, and cutting this into seven equal lengths, she laid them out and said,

"One at a time please select a piece and then share just one special memory, event or experience that has occurred during our time together. One incident that for you personally has touched your heart."

The evocative words we shared bound us forever and I tied the string around my wrist where it remained for many weeks as a constant reminder of the great learning experience that our voyage had provided, until one day I noticed it was missing. It had finally fallen off and vanished.

At the airport I lined up to check in for the final stages of this journey.

It was chaotic inside the terminal for the air was filled with the sound of crying babies and the noise echoed around the building and it was totally deafening.

This was the period when adoptions from Romanian orphanages were at their height and the flights out of Moscow were packed with American couples clutching these small bundles, all desperate to leave and get home.

Llyn had made a return trip New York/Moscow block booking for five of us and because of the visa delay I had no option but to meet her there on the outward journey.

But what I had failed to mention, and had not focused on myself because I had been so engrossed in other aspects of the trip, was the fact that I had no need to return via New York as my immediate destination once the trip had concluded was my home in England.

During the past days I had been totally living in the present and it was not until I was standing in front of the check-in desk and the clerk seemed to be taking an extra long look at my documents, before she then called a senior supervisor over, that I gave any attention to this return journey.

She had noted that as soon as I arrived in the USA I was booked on the first flight back to England. I now heard her say, "We can transfer you on to a direct flight from here to London. It is one that leaves shortly and we would also be happy to upgrade you to Business Class."

It showed the state of exhaustion I was in, for my brain had totally stopped working. My return journey was encoded and locked in and this cluster of cells could not muster the energy to handle any change of plan.

My voice, however, still worked and it said, "No. Thank you!"

So I boarded an airplane full of exhausted new parents and screaming babies, passed over London and went westward all the way across the Atlantic Ocean, changed airports in the USA and then headed the 3,000 miles all the way back again!

Finally, after a car journey from London back to the city of Winchester, I was happy to fall into the embrace of my family as they welcomed me home.

The events of the past two weeks had been very powerful and tied me forever to my traveling companions. The words I used to tell my family about my globetrotting were somewhat superficial and a veneer that covered the deep effect this trek had had on my heart and soul.

I knew I was not alone in withholding a true reportage of my trip, for along with each of my companions, we experienced a need to enter our caves as we readjusted from the great Siberian Plains to the cacophony of our crowded streets and material world. But with the advent of e-mail we were able to maintain a close contact with each other, which was a great comfort.

For the first few days of adjustment I needed some space. Not only physical and mental, but also on a spiritual level for there had been many mysterious events as well as personal lessons that I needed to relive and review and at the culmination of this mental focus of my journey try to discover the meaning and depth of what I perceived to be many gifts.

It was a very difficult time.

Although I was surrounded by a loving family, there was much I knew that I had to withhold and keep secret. This was not because I had any personal doubt of the strange and powerful events that had touched me so deeply, but a protective move that came with an innate sense that they were not ready to hear of such things, and certainly it would have put my levelheaded husband in fear of my mental stability.

Slowly my life resumed its familiar pattern and I fell back into my role. However, there was a subtle difference for I felt a confidence and a newfound wisdom that I hoped would in time enhance my grandchildren's lives.

The shamans of Tuva share the belief with many people

worldwide that all things happen for a reason. Something many of us living in a very different culture often find difficult to believe and we are unable to accept that painful events are the pathway to greater good.

My faith in these beliefs was brought to the fore shortly after my return when I faced some unwanted news, for before the end of the first week home I learned that two of my close friends had been diagnosed with cancer.

Peter had been a family friend for twenty-five years. He was a man with a healthy approach to life, and he enjoyed himself socially, but also made the effort to keep fit and had run respectable times in both the London and the New York marathons.

Distance and busy lives often meant that we only met up a couple of times a year but we were so comfortable in each other's company that the conversation always seemed to take up where it had been left some months before. These days with the universal use of cell phones and e-mail, contact is more frequent and brief notes make it easy to keep up the rapport.

The other had been a close girlfriend for many years until our lives had diverged and taken us to dwell in different countries, and although news continued to filter through from mutual friends we had not seen each other for a while.

But recently my husband and I had purchased a small apartment back in the area we had grown up in and although we were not living there on a full-time basis, as we had a home in Ireland and also an apartment in Florida, we once again had a residence in this familiar neighborhood.

Lesley had already had major surgery to remove a malignant tumor and was about to embark on her first course of chemotherapy. In our culture this disease of cancer seems to be the plague of the twentieth century and there must be few families who escape untouched by it.

Ten years previously I had undergone a mastectomy to

remove a malignant area from my body, so I had a personal understanding of the trauma such a discovery brings.

Sometimes to provide the role of a good listener can in itself be therapeutic, and I sensed that when Lesley called and I picked up the phone this was what she was in need of at this moment and I was happy to contribute in any way possible.

The conversation ran on and she inquired about my travels and was fascinated to hear the stories of the shamans I had just visited. She asked many questions about the ceremonies, the healing rituals and their beliefs and I could feel she was genuinely interested.

She is a very positive person, who has an inquiring and open mind.

I tend to be reticent and avoid leading the conversation into areas that others may prefer to bypass, but more and more I often find others approach me and instigate the lead into a discussion about shamanism and the metaphysical.

Lesley concluded our conversation by asking if I would perform a healing ritual for her. This I was happy to do and I invited her over. She asked if she could come immediately and was at my home within the hour while I spent that intermediate time in preparation.

In all of my homes I keep a small altar. This is no ostentatious affair. Here it is a selection of items that I deem sacred and have them placed on the top of a small chest in the hallway, just inside the front door where they get passed and acknowledged frequently.

The objects range from stones that have returned with me from special ceremonial places to a little silver statuette of a 'grey alien' figure, a china figure of Mother Mary and also a small bronze statue of Green Tara. There is also a piece of vine from the ayahuasca plant that grows in the Amazon and an assortment of feathers, shells and dried leaves.

The latest additions had been the ashes from the ceremonial

fires that had been lit on the journey through Tuva now contained in a small silver box and alongside this was the hand-carved offering spoon given to me by Moon Heart.

Hanging on the wall above all of this are two photographs, one of an extraordinary crop circle, and the other is one that I personally took of a shaman's room in the Andes after a healing ceremony had taken place, everyone had departed, and the room was empty. Here a strange shaft of bright white light cuts down from high in one corner of the picture and like a celestial beam shines onto a large animal skin on the dirt floor, where each of the patients had taken turns to lie during the healing process.

I stood in front of these artifacts and instinctively selected a few. These items I now placed on a small side table that I had set up in the sitting room as a central focus and where I had already placed a large candle in the center and I also added three red carnations, removing them from an arrangement of flowers already standing in a vase in the room.

Earlier in the day I had passed a market stall, and although unknowing of how the day would unfold had been guided to purchase these blooms, unaware that they would prove to be an important part of the day's already unfolding program.

Constantly I am surprised by how the Universe works; carnations are the chosen flowers that are still used in various ways in healing ceremonies by shamans in most South American countries. Their use goes as far back as memory extends and it is accepted without question that they possess a beneficial healing agent.

One shaman I visited in Ecuador used only the petals mixed with oil, which were rubbed over the patient's body; and a famed Brazilian shaman requests a gift of three carnations before the ritual commences. While another whom I have witnessed doing powerful work uses a piece of string to which she attaches one of these flower heads, and once the healing session is complete the patient is given instructions to wear it as a necklace until all the petals have fallen off.

With these thoughts in my mind, I continued with my own preparation and focused on the healing ritual that was soon to take place.

Into one of the small beautiful bowls that had been gifted to me in Tuva I put some water, added a drop of rose essence and placed this alongside the other items on the table.

Next I went out into the garden and picked a few small stems from one of the shrubs, remembering before I cut them to first request permission from the spirit of the shrub. While still outside I threw bread to the four directions, silently aligning myself with the natural elements, the powers of Nature and mentally asking my guides that I be used as a healing channel.

Back indoors I lit the candle and once it was burning brightly I sat down, picked up my drum and the beater and keeping the sound low and regular I focused my thoughts on my friend, now on her way here. I requested my spirit guides and helpers to join me, and there was an instant response and my skin prickled as I felt them draw close.

Lesley arrived and after brief hugs and hellos we agreed to go straight into the healing ritual and keep all our chatting and family news until this was finished.

My intent was to become a conduit for the unseen healing energies that surround us, to funnel them towards this lady who was seeking help.

From past experience I knew that it was not necessary to be deep in the Amazon Jungle or in the high Himalayas for extraordinary things to take place. I knew if it were meant to happen, this healing ritual taking place in a small apartment in a county city would be no less successful because of its location.

From all of the shamanic healing ceremonies I had witnessed and participated in over the past few years I collated my own version; I followed my heart and the internal voice that I felt came from my spirit guides and ancestors.

My actions were instinctive. I just did what felt right and with the use of smoke and water, stones and plants, eggs and feathers and right intention the energies of the patient were cleansed and revitalized.

On completion Lesley sealed the actions with her approval.

She simply said, "Hmmmm. That felt GOOD."

Later after cups of tea and a rekindling of our long friendship she prepared to leave and I gave her one of the Khata scarves to take home, telling her it was a gift from the land of Tuva.

"Do I wear it?" she asked.

I replied, "When you get home just hold it close for a few minutes and see what thoughts come into your head. You will be guided to know where it should go."

Then in a final gesture I removed the heads from the three carnations and told her to take them with her, to dig a small hole in her garden and bury them.

It was just three days later that my husband and I met up with our other friend who was undergoing his own battle with this disease. He had lost all of his hair and was physically frail, but his spirit was strong and he was facing his next round of chemical treatment with great courage and fortitude. We met for lunch, which was a million miles away from dreary; it was full of fun with much gossip and laughter.

As we departed I handed him one of the two remaining Khata scarves which I had gift wrapped, telling him briefly what the package contained and that it had been present at powerful healing ceremonies in Siberia, which I felt had imbued it with healing energies and I knew it was meant for him.

Again came the question as to where he should place it and again I responded with the words, "You will know. Just follow your heart."

A letter from him a couple of days later informed me that it was kept under his pillow and now sharing the bed with him and his lovely wife.

By return I wrote back to them sharing the extraordinary story of an identical Khata scarf I had received three years earlier.

The one I referred to had been an exchanged gift from his Holiness the Dalai Lama when, with a small group of friends during a visit to Ladakh, we had been privileged to have a private audience with him in his home in Dharamsala.

This story started in the home that I have in a remote area of Ireland and began the week before I set off for India.

For a brief period I was living alone in this house and on seven consecutive mornings prior to my departure I had been given the most unusual and unrequested alarm call.

The first time it had been a continuous tapping on the bedroom window that had awakened me. I drew back the curtains to be confronted by a large black raven. He sat on the outside sill, quizzically tipping his head to one side, just looking at me for a few minutes, before with a flap of his wings he flew away.

That first morning I explained it away by the probability that he was confused by his reflection, but he reappeared without fail at a similar time each morning and I would awaken to this urgent tapping.

He was there come rain or shine.

One morning I was already awake and had returned to the bed with a cup of tea, the curtains were drawn back open and as I sat there I saw him arrive. He flew in, landed, closed down his wings and peered in before once again repeating his ritual. I stared at him as he tapped loudly away on the glass; his bright eyes sparkling and his head turned looking directly at me.

During this week before I left, the entrance and driveway to my home were receiving major repairs and while this work was being carried out my car had been moved out of the way and was parked in the grounds of my nearest neighbor which is about a ten-minute walk away. When I walked up to collect it prior to my drive to the airport on the first stage of my journey to Delhi, this neighbor Mike wished me a safe journey then added,

"Your car has been receiving a lot of attention this week. A large black bird has insisted in sitting on it and although our family's three cars have been parked alongside, it wasn't interested in any of those.

It was very strange and as fast as we shooed him off he'd return!

My son has had to continually hose it down to keep removing its droppings."

My travels though India and Ladakh were full of mysterious, metaphysical events and there seemed to be a continuous presence of large black birds to witness all that happened.

While in Leh I had asked Lama Ji, a monk who was accompanying us on our journey, if their presence had any meaning or significance. He had looked at me deeply and affirmed that the raven had long been known as a sacred messenger but left it at that.

At the end of my visit there and within twenty-four hours of my return to the West I was shown that even in the center of London this mysterious bird continues to perform these tasks.

The climax of our trip, after visiting many temples and remote monasteries in this exotic land, came shortly before the trip ended, when my companions and I had the honor of meeting his Holiness the Dalai Lama.

After participating in a ceremony led by him in Leh, we 'by chance' shared his plane as he returned to his base in Dharamsala, and a day later in his own home there we were given the privilege of a private audience.

This amazing man who is in touch with state leaders and concerned with world affairs maintains a humility that has not removed him from the day to day basic needs and problems of the rest of us. But he is full of joy, and the abiding memory of all who meet him is his sense of fun and his love of life.

The traditional way of greeting between Tibetans when you

visit them at home is the exchange of the Khata scarf.

This scarf is a length of white silk, fringed at each end, and the weave is patterned with ancient Buddhist symbols. These scarves are for sale everywhere, on little market stalls by the side of the road, from peddlers walking in and out of the alleys, and in most of the one-room, but numerous, stores.

The local houses are festooned with them, draped over windows and doorways; they hang from every conceivable point.

These days they can be as small as 12 inches by 48 inches and made of a cheap synthetic material, but size and weave is unimportant. It is the thought behind the gesture that has the value of this exchange, and as with all cultures the time-honored tradition is to wish each other well: "What I wish for myself, I wish for you" or "May blessings be on your home and on your family". The silent exchange of a Khata scarf enhances or even replaces the verbal greeting used by other nationalities.

On our walk to and prior to entering the gated compound where his Holiness resides we had been directed by Lama Ji to each purchase one of these scarves and as our audience with the Dalai Lama came to an end we each in turn filed up to him, our forearms outstretched with this symbolic item draped across. The Dalai Lama first placed both of his hands on our head giving a blessing, before lifting up the scarf from our arms which he then gently placed around our necks.

When this final act was completed we moved outside where he posed for a group photo with all of us wearing our precious new scarves.

What a memento to take back to our homes!

A physical reminder of our time spent with this unique man and a permanent keepsake to adorn and make a focal point in our own homes.

This was not our only gift, for His Holiness had arranged for us to visit another highly respected Lama where another ceremony, calling on the blessing of Green Tara, would be performed on our behalf. This gift would come from a man who had been his tutor and lived just a short walk away in this small settlement.

The town of Dharamsala is the hub of all Tibetan activities outside of their ancestral homeland. At 5,000 feet in the foothills of the Himalayas it is an area of outstanding natural beauty. A huge variety of trees grow here and the occasional bright splash of yellow from an indigenous shrub intersperses every shade of green.

The narrow road approaching this unique place winds around and around as you drive ever upwards. It is unfenced and the land falls steeply away to reveal deep tree-filled gorges.

Dharamsala, sited in the north of India, is full of international seekers of the mystical rather than the casual tourist, but is none the less a little Tibet. Whether they are monks in their yellow and saffron robes or shopkeepers wearing traditional costume, their features declare that they are exiles from the Land of Snow, having been ousted from their homeland by the Chinese.

It was in this awesome setting that we entered this revered Lama's dwelling, where we were greeted by two smiling monks and shown to a large outside terrace, before they silently disappeared.

There was a roof covering but two sides were open to the elements and the feeling of being suspended prevailed as we became aware of the sheer drop on both sides.

We were hundreds of feet above the valley floor, and at eye level a flock of large black birds floated on the thermals as we gazed out at this breathtaking view.

A short while later, the monks returned and moved between us holding large jugs and trays of cups offering us the traditional butter tea, before once again withdrawing.

Wherever I travel it constantly amazes me that the less material possessions that people own, the greater the hospitality and what little they do have is always generously shared.

A large carpet covered most of the stone floor of this terrace. Now aged and faded it still held traces of its beauty. The weave must originally have been bright blues and reds, but the pattern of a mandala, a symbolic Tibetan design, remained.

On the two walls hung several tankas made from beautiful silks, all hand painted and embroidered with images of powerful deities. An ornate gilt-framed chair padded with a large cushion, with a footstool set in front of it and raised on a small dais, was at one end of the area and this was the only piece of furniture.

After about ten minutes of simply soaking in the magnificence of the view, the two monks appeared once more. They moved between our group and bowed to each of us as they retrieved our empty cups.

Minutes later a hush fell over our chattering group as a small portly gentleman clad in monk's robes walked in, bowed to us and then seated himself on the chair. His arrival was announced in no way other than his presence, but such was his aura it called for attention.

He bowed to us once more and then seated himself on the chair where, with a gentle hand signal, he indicated for us also to sit down.

I noticed the other two monks quietly slip back in and they too seated themselves on the floor just inside the door.

The atmosphere felt charged as this man commenced the ceremony and started chanting in his ancient language as he called on the love and compassion of Green Tara. And once more we knew we were blessed to be able to participate in yet another memorable event as this high ranking lama called on the energies of the Goddess and in particular on her healing powers.

The intermittent striking of brass bowls by his two assistants added to the atmosphere as the presence of this deity was invoked, and the request was made that she protect us and aid in healing with either physical or emotional problems.

We understood no words of this ritual, steeped as it was in

ancient mystical tradition and spoken in the Tibetan dialect, but the sound vibrated through my very being, a sound that felt as if it would continue on into eternity.

Additional background chanting from the monks who had been our attentive waiters accompanied all of this, and every one of us sat immobile with our legs folded and our heads bowed, the blessed Khata scarves still hanging around our necks.

It was a moment of timelessness.

Finally the throwing of rice and the lavish sprinkling of water over us concluded the ceremony and brought our time here to a close.

The experience seeped deep into our souls, encompassing the whole group, uniting us a whole and we were all deeply moved.

How could one fail to be touched by this most memorable day?

It was a climatic conclusion to our journey.

The following day we were back in Delhi and the day after that I had said goodbye to all of my newfound friends and was sitting on a plane, heading for England.

The precious Khata scarf was lovingly wrapped and placed in my hand luggage for safekeeping and I was just sitting quietly, my head free from any particular thoughts or plans.

Suddenly, without warning, a voice loud and clear but coming from inside my head said,

"You must give the scarf to Lyn."

I did know someone called Lyn, but there was an immutable sense that this was not the Lyn the voice was referring to, and I was totally unaware of the identity of the soon to be recipient. However, this fact did not seem to present a problem.

There was also no trace of any reluctance from me to part with this unique item, but a complete acceptance of the order.

I arrived at Heathrow Airport in England in mid-afternoon, where my husband Barry met me and we drove into London for a brief overnight stop, with our plans made to continue on to

Ireland early the following morning.

It had been a good many hours and a time change since I had left central Delhi. I felt very weary and was looking forward to a shower, hair wash and a sleep.

My son Daniel, who was now living in this city, would be joining us for dinner that evening and I wanted to be alert enough to enjoy his company.

Barry's voice, as he shared what he'd been up to in the past three weeks since we'd last been together in an effort to bring me up-to-date, floated around the cab, but most of what he was relating was drifting past me.

It was a world away from the mountains and monks of the Himalayas, the ceremonies and the strange events that had surrounded me on that journey and I tried to assimilate myself back into the London metropolis.

Suddenly like a bolt from the blue the word *Lyn* leapt out of his monologue.

It brought me out of my reverie and he instantly had my attention.

"What was that you were saying? Tell me again!" I insisted and he patiently repeated the story.

He owns a couple of racehorses and the previous day, with the trainer and also a couple of other owners, he had been out on the gallops watching them as they worked.

It appeared that one of the ladies present owned a horse that would be running in a meeting at Ascot Racecourse in a week's time, the same day as his horse was running there.

I continued listening as he told me:

"I expect you'll meet her there. Her name is Caroline. Oops! It's not! I must remember it's Caro*lyn*. She's very particular about it. While I was there she turned to Mickey (the man who trains both of these horses) and said...

'You have known me for ten years. Will you please stop calling me Caroline? I keep telling you my name is Caro*lyn*.'"

Instantly I knew that this was the person for whom the scarf was intended and any doubt was removed as Barry continued his story.

"As we stood there waiting for the horses to come up the hill I saw she had a back problem and had great difficulty walking. She was leaning heavily on her sister and before long had to be helped back into the car. Her sister rejoined the rest of us and we continued to watch the horses go through their paces.

I asked her if Carolyn had suffered a slipped disc, to which she replied,

'I wish it were that simple; sadly, it's a lot more serious than that.'"

Instantly, the voice within my head confirmed that this was the lady who was to be the recipient of the Khata scarf and I could pass it on within a matter of days.

We arrived at the hotel, checked in and got to our room where I immediately took a shower and then fell into bed.

As I closed my eyes I thought, "That's perfect, I know whom the scarf is for. I'll be meeting her next week and I can give it to her then."

I prepared for sleep, but it was impossible. Into my head, and coming in loud and clear, was a voice giving me further instructions.

It was totally bizarre, for a dialogue then ensued between this voice from an unknown source and me.

VOICE: "*She needs it now!*"

ME: "I'll do it next week. I can't do anything now."

VOICE: "*Yes you can.*"

ME: "I can't. It's 4.30 p.m. Daniel's arriving shortly to spend the evening with us and I leave again at 7.30 a.m. tomorrow morning. I want to sleep."

VOICE: "*Wake up! Get her address. You can post it.*"

ME: "I'm too tired!"

VOICE: "*Do it now!*"

Its demands were impossible to ignore.

Reluctantly, I hauled myself out of bed, walked into the sitting area and said to my husband,

"Would you do me a favor? Please could you ring Mickey and get the address of this lady called Carolyn?"

One look at my bleary eyes told him it was pointless to question why.

He simply said, "Sure, go back to bed."

Thankfully I slipped once again beneath the covers. I heard him make the call and was aware that he had then come into the bedroom and I heard him say,

"I've written it down. It's on the bedside table."

I was waiting for sleep to come.

Instead there were further instructions from this androgynous voice as it demanded:

"*Sit up!*" And the conversation continued.

ME: "Please let me sleep. I'll put the scarf in an envelope when I wake up and ask the hotel reception to post it for me."

VOICE: "*Wake up! Look at the address!*"

It was so demanding I had no choice. With great difficulty I reluctantly obeyed the order and sat up, opened my eyes and picked up the slip of paper.

The name of this lady's house was **Raven Court** and she lived in a town about thirty miles outside the capital.

The incredible synchronicity in the name of the black bird that had been stalking me for the past three weeks was even more confirmation that this was indeed the person for whom the precious scarf was intended.

But the voice had still not finished with me, for now it demanded:

"*Phone her!*"

Finally I accepted that there would be no sleep until every act this voice demanded had been completed and I did as it requested.

Carolyn answered the phone and my introduction went something like this,

"Carolyn. My name is Wendy. We've never met, but I'm aware that you have a problem with your back. I've just returned from India where I met with the Dalai Lama and I have a small silk scarf he gave me, which I was also wearing at an auspicious ceremony honoring the Green Tara Goddess.

I feel very strongly that it contains healing energies and I know beyond any doubt that it is a gift from him to you. I am merely the courier.

It is your choice what you do with it and whether you wear it or simply keep it in your pocket. My part of the exercise is almost finished.

I'm staying overnight at the Connaught Hotel in London and I'm going to put it in one of their envelopes and post it to you. It should arrive within a couple of days."

There was a short silence, and then I heard her say,

"Thank you so much. Do you think you could take it into my office? I'll be there first thing in the morning."

By this time it was about five o'clock.

"Carolyn, I'm so sorry," I said, "but right now I just don't have the time."

Her response left me dumbstruck.

There was a sense of The Divine in action and I felt my skin prickle and my hair stand on end as I heard her say:

"My office is in the same street as the Connaught Hotel. It's in the basement below the estate agents."

I stepped out of bed, walked the few feet to the window and glanced out.

There, directly opposite and less than 100 feet away from me, was a window displaying photographs of houses and the sign above the window read Strutt & Co. Estate Agents!

Within five minutes the article in question was safely on her desk and I was back in bed.

Now with my mission complete, the voice departed and I was allowed to sink into a wonderful restful sleep.

This special and true story I have shared with many people since it occurred, but it has never lost one ounce of its magic or power, and serves constantly to remind me how amazing our lives can be.

Hope is a precious emotion and one that can pull us through the darkest days.

But right now back in Winchester there was still one remaining Khata scarf. It was folded neatly on one side of the altar and for a week I looked at it daily, knowing it would not remain there for long. There was no question in my mind that it belonged to someone else.

I was simply the messenger, at present unaware of its destination and recipient.

The call finally came.

Chapter 11

The specific call I had been waiting for arrived a few days later. Once again it was via the telephone and again from Lesley, but the news she shared with me was not what I had been expecting and shocked me to my core.

For many weeks my friend had kept secret the knowledge that her daughter also had cancer.

Mandy, her eldest child, had only a couple of months previously given birth to her first baby and what should have been a joyous time was now totally overshadowed by this news.

This young woman was not only facing fears for her own life, but the additional, overwhelming and unspoken one was that there was a possibility her son would lose his mother before he even grew to know her.

It was a scenario that shocked and rocked the lives of this extended family at its very foundation and was almost too much to bear.

I had first met her when she was just a child, a gentle caring girl and a real animal lover who had been a strict vegetarian since her early teens. At this point the very idea of receiving chemotherapy and radiotherapy horrified her. The sheer thought of the destructive action that this invasive treatment would perform on the cells of her body went against every belief she held.

We are all so very different. Within a family we accept the physical differences readily, but our emotional attitudes to adversity even within the same genetic pool for whatever reason are frequently at opposite ends of the scale.

In her confusion she had lost sight of the battle on hand and her thoughts were consumed and focused on the fact that her body was about to be filled with toxins.

The healing ceremony that Lesley had received had left this

lady with a positive feeling of upliftment and she had persuaded Mandy to see me in the hope that somehow she could face this treatment with a more positive attitude, and was now asking if I could go to her home and perform a similar ceremony for her daughter.

I lost no time in gathering a few sacred items from my altar before getting in my car and heading for her home, stopping only at the florist to purchase some red carnations.

It had been quite a while since I had last seen Mandy, certainly it was before she had got married, but again time had not erased nor diminished the same rapport with her as I had felt with her mother.

The three of us sat together in the large sunny family kitchen and I tried to soothe away her very obvious concerns and worries.

I explained how I would be calling on the unseen energies of our planet and I spoke about Guardian Angels, reminding her of how we all survive hair-raising escapades as children and likened my belief in spirit guides to these protective entities. Keeping the conversation light I tried to allay any trepidation she had about a ceremony by keeping my voice low, quietly listening to her worries and watching as her breathing slowed and she began to relax.

Next I set out the items I had carried with me onto the table and lit a candle. Leaving Mandy watching the flame I went out into the garden and quickly 'journeyed' to my guides seeking fuel for my intent.

Returning into the house I gave her a big smile and said,
"We're ready."

Hearing these words Lesley excused herself and went out of the room, quietly shutting the door behind her.

Asking Mandy to stand I took a deep breath, focused my thoughts and reached out to touch her. The moment I laid my hands lightly on her shoulders I felt every hair on my body stand up and I knew in an instant that a spirit entity had drawn very close.

Immediately I became aware of who it was that had swept in, and there was not the slightest doubt... it was her grandmother, her maternal grandmother.

It was such a powerful sensation that I was experiencing. This sense of knowing is so strong for me and was no less than if this lady's physical living body was standing alongside me and I immediately shared this information with Mandy.

Apart from an "Oh!" from the patient on hearing my statement, the healing continued without conversation, the only sound coming from the bird song as it floated in through the open window as they enjoyed a beautiful summer day.

I was guided by an unseen hand throughout the healing ritual, and apart from that initial touching on the shoulders my own hands remained a few inches away from Mandy's body and a smooth, gentle force that tingled and felt almost electrical emitted from my palms and seemed to be focusing on her back.

I felt more like an observer while this was happening, but all the while I was very aware of the grandmother remaining with us; in my mind's eye I could see her clearly. This lady had a beautiful smile on her face and she was holding a pink baby's bonnet which was clearly a knitted one and of a style that has not been fashionable for many years.

Finally I felt the healing energy, which had continually like a gentle electrical current rippled through me, lasting about 10–15 minutes, now begin to dissipate and cease.

I knew this healing session was over.

Directing Mandy to shred some carnation petals into the small bowl of water that was set on the table, I suggested that as she did this she visualize all of her pains and worries about her treatment being dropped into the water.

After a few moments of watching them float and drift around, I scooped the petals back up, wrapped them in a small piece of cloth and gave them back to her with the instruction that she should take them home and, reminding her to first ask permission from the earth before she did so, bury them in her garden.

As I passed the bundle to her there was another subtle shift in the energy in that room and I knew the tangible essence of her grandmother had moved off and had again departed from this realm.

Excusing myself for a moment I picked up the bowl of water and took it outside, and with a prayer of thanks to the unseen spirits I poured it on the ground, offering it to the roots of a rosebush.

As I re-entered the kitchen we were once again joined by Lesley, and also her other daughter, Mandy's sister Keely, who had arrived while we were working.

The shift in Mandy's demeanor from just a short while ago was astonishing… She looked different, less troubled and lighter as if a physical load had been lifted from her shoulders. Now the words just bubbled out of her as she regaled her family with the information that her grandmother had joined us. I added a little to it and shared the information that she had been holding a pink knitted baby's bonnet, the sort that grandmothers years ago spent some of their leisure time making.

Then it was Mandy's turn to share a family story with me.

This lady who had been the rock of the family died several years ago. When her time was imminent most of them had gathered at the family home, but Mandy was away, out of this country and traveling. In those days before the availability of cell phones, she was unable to be contacted and had not received any notice to warn her of this impending event. For that reason she was the only one of the grandchildren not present.

That night, hundreds of miles away and while asleep, she had a vivid dream. In it she dreamed she was in bed and woke up to find her grandmother had come to visit her and was now standing by the side of the bed, saying to her, "I'm leaving now!"

Still in this dream Mandy got out of bed and walked down the stairs with her. As she let her out of the front door she leaned forward and kissed this lady saying, "Good-bye. See you soon." Her grandmother's reply puzzled her for the response was, "No, dear. I won't see you again. This time I won't be coming back."

The dream was so intense that the images from it had dominated her thoughts throughout the morning. At lunchtime that day she was contacted by her family and given the news that her grandmother had died during the night.

Mandy now said, "I often feel her around, but have never spoken of this to anyone. You have made me so happy, because now I know it is not just my imagination."

We exchanged hugs all around, and then I gathered up my bundle of sacred stones and precious items. These throughout the healing ceremony had been sitting on the remaining Khata scarf and I now put them carefully into my bag. This last silk item I lifted up and placed into Mandy's hands saying, "This gift has come from Tuva. It has been present at many powerful healing ceremonies. I know I was merely the courier and it was meant for you. Put it in your home wherever you feel is its rightful place."

I drove home, deep in thought. I knew that whatever I had seen, whatever I had learned during my trip through Siberia, down to Tuva and back had been a personal bonus, for with the passing over of the third and final Khata scarf I knew I had completed my mission.

Once again I had been a messenger of the gods.

The following day there was even more to amaze me and stun me with the endless possibilities of this world we are merely passing through.

As I casually flipped through one of the current day's national newspapers there was an item and picture that stopped me in my tracks: the article was about a film due to have its premiere in a few days' time.

The title of the film was *Signs*; it starred Mel Gibson and showed a copy photo of a still clip from this as yet unseen movie. A movie that told the story of a family making contact with alien beings from a place light years away.

The image was of this very well-known actor and two children. They were sitting together posing for the camera and they were all wearing identical 'homemade' hats... Hats that were made from silver foil with an extremely large pointed top, the same shape as a witch's hat except they had very small turned-up brims and were more like poor copies of the one I had worn during our final shamanic ceremony when the young Russian man felt I was being used to channel energies from some far-off planet.

The beautiful high-coned silver hat worn during that ceremony was now sitting on a side table in this very room!

My hair stood on end as I read the resumé of this yet to be released film... It told the story of a farmer who discovers a series of crop circles in his cornfield and becomes convinced that the phenomena are as a result of extraterrestrial life and he and his children try to connect and communicate with these alien beings.

The moral of the story the article said was that 'everything happens for a reason', something that is one of my mantras.

I made a note to see this film as soon as it arrived at our local cinema. I had no doubt it would not be long before there was a screening, for this area in the south of England where I lived had for many years been the center of worldwide crop circle activity.

Later that day I had a phone call from Lesley and as we chatted I for some reason got up from where I was sitting and walked across to the window. I continued listening to my friend as I watched the traffic passing by. This apartment that we have in England is on the second floor and the room I was in looks down on one of the city's busiest roads.

I listened to her as she told me how she had just returned from a walk on the beach and while she was out had strongly felt the presence of her long-deceased father.

On returning to her home, she had been drawn to take out a small box in which she had kept a few personal mementoes of him. In it was a small diary that had been his and I listened as I heard her say, "I thumbed through it but there was only one entry and it said: 'Visited Lesley today'."

She asked me what I thought and did it mean anything? All I could do was reassure her that the spirit of her father was indeed close and what an amazing way to give her this proof. But as I spoke to her, the familiar prickling of my skin signified a spirit presence had moved close to me. However, I said nothing, for I was not 100% sure who it was and did not wish to presume it was her beloved dad.

But while I had been listening to her my eyes were focused on watching the action outside of the window, observing the traffic and the passersby. And it was a few minutes before I realized that without any logical reason my physical body seemed to have gone into some sort of repetitive action.

Now I was standing with one foot placed in front of the other and was not only rocking backwards and forwards, shifting my weight from one leg to the other, but had slowly turned in a half circle.

What was even more strange was that without any itch or reason to do so, I found while I continued to hold the phone in my right hand, I had placed my other hand on top of my head and with the palm facing down it was making a gentle and repetitive tapping!

Immediately I felt this was something to do with the gentleman we were focused on and shared what was happening with Lesley, asking if she had any idea what it meant.

She could not come up with any idea and I certainly didn't have one, so for the time being this had to remain a puzzle.

But before we had finished our conversation I felt a great

discomfort around my neck and jaws, which I immediately shared with her and this made sense for I now learned that he had been in hospital for the removal of a growth on his throat, and sadly had died of a heart failure while under the anesthetic.

The following day I would be decamping to my home in Ireland, but we promised to keep in touch via the telephone.

That evening with the day almost over I sat down and switched on the television, and the first image appearing was that of the seashore and a man with a small net catching the edible shrimps that this area is famous for, a place called Morecambe Bay, which is halfway up on the west coast of England. As I watched the screen, suddenly and without warning I once again had the identical uncomfortable physical sensations around my neck and throat that I had felt earlier in the day while talking to Lesley. This time I knew immediately that it meant her father was making his presence felt again, and also this time the name Jack accompanied the feelings.

Once settled in the wilds of Kerry in Ireland, I could write without distraction. I gave priority to this action and immediately began to faithfully record the challenges and mysterious events of the trip through Siberia.

Somehow I knew it was important, but I also accepted that for the time being I had to keep a lot of it secret, to not divulge much of what had occurred, for the knowledge that the revelation of some of the occurrences would have those close to me questioning my sanity.

It would be an uphill task finding the ability to accurately and honestly record it all; however, there was an unquestionable instinct that it was important to write it all down and I had a deep felt understanding that one day the time would be right for it all to be shared.

Many of the ancient prophecies were slowly coming to fruition and our world was changing rapidly.

Way in the future I would receive confirmation that the path I was on was a known, although rarely walked one and many times, often several years ahead, I would read a book detailing shamanic rituals and recognize almost word for word notes in my journal where I had previously written a description of one of my metaphysical experiences.

However, that was in the future and the day after I arrived at this home in Ireland I made my way down to the closest beach, a mile-long strip of sandy shore on the edge of the Atlantic. It is unfailingly beautiful and always different as it changes with the weather.

Today there were no more than a handful of people walking the shoreline and I was lost in my thoughts oblivious to them all. The words "more came… more came" started running through my head, and I then found myself saying them out loud, it was so intrusive.

Then it was "more came beach".

Suddenly I got it!!

Morecambe Beach!

It was the seaside town in England. The one that had been pictured on the television nearly two days ago. I had not yet shared the television image of this place and the name Jack with my friend when I felt the presence of her father. This felt like a message to rectify this omission on my part.

After about an hour's walk I returned home and as soon as I had taken my coat off I dialed Lesley's telephone number. She answered it and within minutes had confirmed that her father's name was indeed Jack and her earliest memories were of them together with their fishing nets in Morecambe Bay.

As we continued our conversation and chatted of other things I found that I had got to my feet. And as before I was looking out of the window at passing cars and once again rocking myself from one foot to the other, and again my left hand was making a gentle tapping motion on the very top of my head.

"Your dad is definitely here with me, Lesley," I said. "What else can you tell me about him?"

I heard the words, "He was a barber," and instantly my whole body vibrated.

This was it!!

There was no question the energy of her father was around me and present at this very moment.

This was what I was doing... performing the actions of a barber as he trimmed hair... the left hand resting on the top of the client's head, lifting it up and down as he worked the scissors in his right hand, all the while moving with tiny rocking steps as he walked around the large chair.

I excitedly shared this information with my friend and the words she added put the icing on the cake for I heard her say, "His shop was on a busy main road and he loved watching out of the large window; he always said, 'I can see the world go by from here!'"

The indisputable knowledge that her much loved, deceased father continued to watch over her provided my friend with great joy. This along with the confirmation that our spirits live on also gave her added strength as she moved into a long and difficult period of treatment for cancer.

My visit to Tuva is a tale of the heart ruling the head and shows how our lives can truly unfold when we allow this to happen.

The magical and non-ordinary events that had repeatedly, but intermittently touched my life during the previous ten years now over the past couple of months appeared to be escalating. This had a profound effect on me, for although they were impossible to explain they proved difficult to dismiss.

They cemented my belief in a unseen dimension that existed beyond our human touch and normal capabilities, and this put an end to the corporate lifestyle I had been living up to this point. Everything changed as I now entered and committed myself to a new phase of my life's journey.

I focused my time and energies on seeking out healers in other small communities living in remote areas of the globe, visiting these people, staying with them, watching and learning from them as I observed how they continually lived in harmony with the natural world and a physically unseen world as they practiced shamanism.

The need to learn more about the 'force' that had engulfed my physical body and overruled all normal control during the Tuvan ceremonies became a priority and for the next ten years I traveled the world.

Over this period I religiously kept a diary recording my extra-ordinary personal experiences. Writing them as honestly as I could and devoid of embellishment. Verbally sharing the recall of the event only with those who had been present and witnesses at the time.

Most of it I kept secret, not because I had any doubt of what I saw and felt, but to protect those who would have filled with fear at the hearing of my tale.

I waited and watched as the Western world slowly opened their eyes, began seeking a reason for their lives and entered a more spiritual approach as this swept across the land. Now I felt the time was right to share my story.

Writing *Two Hearts in Tuva* took me nearly a year. Often I would take a few weeks' break from it and focus on the more recent mystical and extraordinary events that I had been privy to, but always and often reluctantly I was pulled back to continue writing this story.

Often I would question why I was doing it. There were other things I would sometimes have preferred to be doing, and there was no obvious pressure to relate it and no seeking of financial reward.

But there was without question an unseen driving force over the months that did not lessen.

When it was complete I sent the manuscript to Llyn Roberts

to ask her permission to use her true name before I sent it to the publisher.

Three days later we both received the news that Moon Heart had, unbeknownst to us, died suddenly in circumstances that remained unexplained; and that her untimely death had occurred almost a year previously at approximately the same time as I had felt compelled to record the story of my journey with this amazing woman and turn it into a book.

My hair stood on end when I first heard this news, and I felt the sense and acceptance that the spirit of Moon Heart was close to me. This left me in no doubt that she wanted her story to be told and I had been guided throughout the writing by the spirit of this Tuvan woman. She wants the world to know the endless possibilities of truly gifted shamans and I feel honored to have been a vehicle for the amazing Moon Heart.

Moon Books invites you to begin or deepen your encounter with Paganism, in all its rich, creative, flourishing forms.